TROPHY BUCKS
IN ANY WEATHER

Dan Carlson

Published by

krause publications

An Imprint of F+W Publications

700 East State Street • Iola, WI 54990-0001
715-445-2214 • 888-457-2873
www.krausebooks.com

Our toll-free number to place an order or obtain
a free catalog is (800) 258-0929.

Library of Congress Control Number: 2007942694

ISBN-13: 978-0-89689-610-9
ISBN-10: 0-89689-610-2

Front Cover Photograph by Denver Bryan

Designed by Thomas Nelsen
Edited by Derrek Sigler

Printed in China

Acknowledgements

Writing a book about weather and deer hunting is among the most challenging things I've ever done, and certainly not something I could have accomplished alone. Many people have contributed time, effort, graphics and photographs to make this book a reality. I extend special thanks to Dr. Michael Pidwirny and the University of British Columbia Okanagan for help in providing graphics to explain certain weather situations. My thanks to Todd Nordeen, District Wildlife Manager for the Nebraska Game and Parks Commission, for information and photos that he provided, and to South Dakota's Department of Game, Fish and Parks in Rapid City and Pierre for patience in answering my many questions over the years. And special thanks to Amy Sircy, my personal editor and proofreader on this project, for her many hours of help and suggestions.

This book contains many photographs provided by fellow hunters, colleagues, friends and meteorologists who were willing to share stories and images to help me better illustrate the information presented. To each and every one of you, my heartfelt thanks. I thank The Black Hills Pioneer Newspaper in Spearfish, South Dakota, for its support and aid, and Randee Peterson at Blackhills.com for helping through the technical stuff over the years. I also thank meteorologist and photographer Eric A. Helgeson for special assistance in providing key photographs, and the team at the Rapid City National Weather Service Office. Special thanks to Cabela's for believing in me enough to help this project proceed. Thanks to all who prayed for me and the successful completion of this work, and to God for his strength and sustenance to see me through. Finally, thanks to my lovely wife and hunting buddy, Karen, and my two children, Rebekah and Alex, for their support, faith, encouragement and patience when I wrote late into the night and every weekend for three months to bring this book to life.

This book is dedicated to my son Alex, and my daughter, Rebekah, who have chosen to follow the hunter's path with Mom and Dad. I look forward to many more happy hunting seasons with both of you.

Dan Carlson

Contents

Introduction

It was an unseasonably mild Monday morning on November 11, 1940, and even as the first battles of what would be a second World War raged in Europe, hundreds of men and boys in the upper Mississippi River valley decided to celebrate Armistice Day by going duck hunting. Dozens never saw their families again. The weather killed them.

About 50 years after that terrible day a husband and wife were hunting elk in the Black Hills, but no matter what they tried, the elk seemed to be one step ahead of them. Time and again they would stalk up to a ridge or saddle, only to find fresh sign where elk had bedded, or they'd see a fleeting glimpse of a fleeing herd. The weather had betrayed them.

A couple of years later the same two hunters were peeking down rows of corn in search of deer. Each had two tags to fill, one of which had to be an antlerless deer. The husband spotted a large doe bedded halfway down a row, but wondered how they would they get close enough without spooking her. How would his wife put a .270 rifle bullet through the deer's heart at a range of less than 10 yards when all one normally sees hunting deer in corn is white tails waving goodbye as the deer race away down the row? The weather helped them.

The December sky was sunny but cold northwest winds were howling, and wind chill factors were nearing zero in a barren farm field north of South Dakota's Black Hills nearly 10-years later. A lone deer hunter cradled his CVA Optima muzzleloader in his arms as he left his truck intent on filling his tag. Less than 30-minutes later he was standing over the deer that fell where it had been standing when a Powerbelt Aerotip fired from 25-feet away broke its neck. How did he know exactly where a deer would be on such a bitter and windy winter day? The weather told him.

Weather is the most common topic of conversation in the world, and is often the opening line or "ice breaker" that leads to other subjects. Just think of how many times the subject comes up in your own life every day and you'll realize it's true. How many times a day do you begin conversations with a remark about how warm, how cold, how lovely, or how windy the day is? How often do you comment about what the weather is supposed to be like over the coming weekend?

Thanks to the prevalence of TV and radio meteorologists, the Weather Channel and a wealth of information online about weather, we know and understand more about what it is and how Earth's "weather engine" works than ever before. But one area of weather that has remained largely unexplored is the role it plays in big-game animal behavior and how hunters can use that knowledge to their advantage.

I was a weathercaster and meteorologist for TV, radio and print media for more than 20 years, and I've been a hunter for 30 years. During that time I have come to understand how deer and other game animals react to certain weather situations and why. I have no trophy entries in any record books and no stunning mounts on my wall. I hunt primarily for the joy of the experience and for the nutritious meat it puts on my table. But whether you're a meat hunter like me, or looking to bag the buck of a lifetime, you might want to consider what's in the pages ahead. It's primarily because of the information they contain that I've never failed to fill my tag and bring home venison in the last 15 years.

CHAPTER 1

Weather 101

There are certain risks a guy takes when he decides to be a TV weatherman, not the least of which is the forfeiture of any privacy in a public place. Every day, wherever a TV weather presenter goes, there will be one question asked by almost everyone he or she comes in contact with, and that's "What's the weather?" My admittedly tongue-in-cheek response to that question obviously seeking a personal weather forecast was, "The weather is the observed state of the atmosphere, as expressed in meteorological terminology, at a specific geographic location at a precise point in time."

For our purposes, that's exactly what we'll be talking about as we relate weather conditions to the behavior of deer and other big-game animals. We will be talking about what the weather is doing at the treestand, at the ground blind, at the farm field and on the mountain where you are pursuing your quarry.

Meteorology, or the scientific study of weather, can be extremely complex and involve all kinds of mathematics, physics, chemistry, geography, hydrology and other disciplines I call "*ICKs*" and "*EEs*." They can be fascinating to some but unnecessarily boring to those of us who just

The atmosphere is barely visible in this photograph of Earth as a thin blue hazy border glowing on the outer edge of the planet.
Photo courtesy of NASA.
Public domain.

want to know what that big blue "H" over our hunting ground on the Weather Channel weather map means for our hunt the next morning. For that reason, I'm going to keep things as simple and practical as possible in my discussion of basic weather principles, but there are some fundamentals that must be understood.

Though there are five primary levels of the atmosphere that extend from the ground all the way up to the outermost regions thousands of miles overhead, 75% of the atmosphere's mass and pretty much everything that has to do with hunting weather takes place in the lowest 5-8 miles called the troposphere. This layer of air where all the action takes place is pretty thin compared to the relative size of the planet.

When viewed from space, the visible portion of our atmosphere shows up only as a very narrow halo of blue surrounding Earth. As a rough and basic comparison, the depth of the troposphere relative to the size of our planet is less than the thickness of the paper that the maps wrapped around a 12" globe are printed on.

Our understanding of weather and how it works has increased exponentially since the Second World War. The invention of radar, aircraft and rockets capable of flight above the troposphere into the stratosphere and beyond, computers able to crunch massive amounts of numerical data into understandable weather maps, improved ground sensor arrays, instantaneous global communication, weather satellites, and increased interest in weather on behalf of the public have all greatly contributed to the accuracy of weather forecasts and improved advance warning of dangerous weather conditions. Prior to World War II we had almost no understanding of what we now call the jet stream or how it influenced the courses of weather systems that create conditions at ground level. It was only after high-flying German and American pilots discovered sharp discrepancies between the indicated airspeed on their instruments and measured ground speed that these meandering rivers of high-speed winds overhead were discovered and deemed important.

Airmen serving aboard high-flying aircraft such as the B-29 Superfortress during World War II were among the first to recognize the importance of learning more about the jet stream.
Photo by author.

Depending where you are on the planet, the prevailing wind direction overhead varies. In the continental United States our weather systems predominantly move from a general west-to-east direction, but seldom do they move precisely from west to east. Storm systems and the mystical "upper level disturbances" forecasters talk about tend to ride with the flow of primary jet streams. Though smaller corridors of higher wind speed are found at any level of the troposphere, even down to ground level, the big low-pressure storm systems responsible for our most dramatic weather events ride either the mid-latitude jet stream (sometimes called the polar jet stream) or sub-tropical jet stream. The mid-latitude jet stream is the more influential of the two on American weather. Depending on the time of year, this atmospheric river that separates cold, dry Canadian air to the north from the South's more temperate and more humid air masses can be positioned anywhere from the southern Canadian provinces to the Gulf Coast.

During the mid-summer the mid-latitude jet stream is usually flowing west to east along the Canadian border. In winter months, it's ever- changing and undulating course can form deep bends southward that permit Canadian air

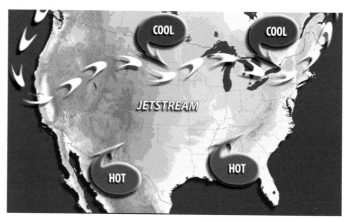

A typical summertime jet stream pattern. Graphic courtesy of AccuWeather at www.accuweather.com. Used by permission.

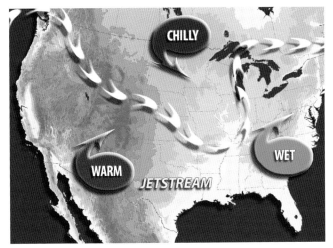

A typical spring or fall jet stream pattern. Jet Stream graphic courtesy of AccuWeather at www.accuweather.com. Used by permission.

to penetrate as far south as Florida and Texas resulting in citrus-damaging freezes and ice storms in the South.

Large dips in the jet stream over the United States are called upper-level or long-wave troughs and often are associated with stormy, active weather changes. This was the case with the jet stream pictured immediately above. A low-pressure system and associated fronts riding along its course spawned a number of tornadoes across eastern Texas and the southern states. When sections of the jet stream take on the shape of an inverted "U," the area inside it is considered under an upper-level ridge and the weather is generally fair and mild during fall and winter months, or scorching hot in the summer.

Fall and spring are the most active weather periods for the United States because they are the seasons in which the atmosphere is in seasonal transition. They are times when severe or extreme weather changes are most likely, and they also coincide with hunting seasons. Understanding how certain weather conditions and changes influence the behavior of deer and other big-game animals is important, especially for hunters who only have a few days in which to fill a tag and must therefore be prepared to hunt in a wide range of weather situations. Failure to anticipate weather changes and what they mean will not only reduce your chances of returning with a deer or limit of birds, but it can also kill you.

The great Armistice Day storm of November 11, 1940, remains one of the deadliest tragedies in the history of hunting in North America and a good example of what I mean. Many people had the day off for the holiday, and waterfowl hunters by the hundreds headed out during an

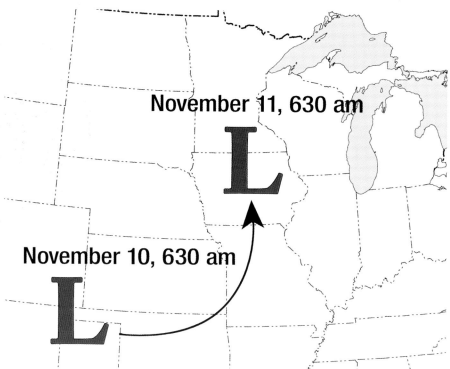

During the 24 hours preceding the dramatic change in weather across the Upper Mississippi Valley in November of 1940, a deep low-pressure center moved from the Texas/Oklahoma Panhandle area into north-central Iowa, keeping southeast Minnesota and western Wisconsin on the mild side of a major storm. Change was sudden and dramatic as the storm center moved through the area. Photo courtesy of the National Weather Service.

unseasonably mild morning across the upper Mississippi River Valley. According to National Weather Service records from LaCrosse, Wisconsin, temperatures around sunrise were near 50 degrees. Hunters from eastern Minnesota across Wisconsin headed for their blinds and duck boats in light jackets. In spite of the mild conditions the hunting was good ... too good. If only those hunters had realized that the huge flocks of waterfowl overhead were not simply migrating, but fleeing what was to come in search of shelter, perhaps more would have survived nature's onslaught.

Early in my weather forecasting career I learned a number of weather proverbs pertaining to animals and birds. Not all such proverbs are true 100% of the time, but often there are tidbits of wisdom in such sayings. One I committed to memory was, "When the goose flies high, fair weather is nigh. When the goose flies low, prepare for a blow." That's one all outdoors enthusiasts should understand, and precisely what was happening on that dreadful day back in 1940.

The hunters didn't understand that the waterfowl they were shooting at were a sign of imminent danger. The low-flying birds were responding to sharply dropping barometric pressure as a deep storm center moved over the area. It began to rain. Winds increased suddenly as a cold front swept across the area. A morning of hunting enjoyment turned to a fight for survival as whitecaps swamped duck boats and rain turned to snow while temperatures tumbled. Many soaked hunters, unable to make it to shore, sought shelter on small islands that dot that stretch of the Mississippi River. Before noon a mild morning with temperatures in the low to mid 50s

had turned into a raging blizzard with 50-80 mph winds, temperatures near 20 degrees, and subzero wind chill factors. The storm claimed more than 150 lives across the Upper Midwest, 49 of them in Minnesota alone. Of those 49, nearly half were ill-prepared hunters found frozen in the storm's wake.

That deadly storm was riding a bend in the mid-latitude jet stream that curved northeast from the Oklahoma Panhandle to western Wisconsin. East of the storm center, east and south of the jet stream, the weather was mild and pleasant. Behind the storm center, north and west of the jet stream, cold air was invading across the Dakotas. The storm itself was working like an agitator in a mixing bowl, throwing warm and moist air north and westward while drawing cold polar air down and east. Most of the major weather-producing systems that big-game hunters will face in the fall seasons will come in the form of low-pressure systems and their associated fronts steered along by the jet stream.

The weather conditions over your hunting ground will be dominated by one of three things: a high-pressure area, a low-pressure system or a state of transition between the two. Stay with me now, I promise to keep things simple.

You may not realize just how strong you are. Scientists have decided that standard atmospheric pressure at sea level is 29.92 inches of mercury, or about 14.7 pounds-per-square-inch. We don't stop to think that air weighs anything, but it does. When your barometer reads 29.92, every square inch of your body's surface has 14.7 pounds pushing against it. I won't bore you with the math, but will entertain you with a couple of examples. A 5'11" man weighing 200 pounds has approximately 24 tons of air exerting pressure on his body from the outside when the barometer reads 29.92 inches. A 5'5" woman weighing 135 pounds has about 19 tons of pressure on her when the barometer reads the same. That perspective adds new meaning to "a person under a lot of pressure." Now let's take this from something mildly interesting to information that's very interesting.

Humans are mammals. So are deer, elk, moose, antelope and other delicious creatures. Mammals are made up of fluid-filled cells that have flexible outer membranes. This is necessary to keep mammals like us from exploding or imploding when there are large changes in atmospheric pressure. I've had some fellow meteorologists scoff at me when I suggest that animals are capable of weather prediction, but stop and think about this for a moment.

Have you ever noticed how certain injuries you might have had start to ache when a change in weather is predicted? Maybe it's an old football knee injury, irritated scar tissue around the incision left from an operation or a healed area around a bone you broke some years back that begins to throb. The next time you experience this, check the barometric pressure readings for the day. Chances are the weatherman will say on the evening news that "the pressure is falling." Your aches and pains from past injuries flare up when pressure falls quickly because the cell structure of scar tissue is less flexible than that of healthy tissue. The difference in the rate of cellular expansion causes your discomfort. I remember my mother used to be able to predict the onset of rain with uncanny accuracy based on which of her joints afflicted with rheumatoid arthritis hurt the most. Now let's take this information into the animal kingdom.

Is it unreasonable to believe that wild animals with senses far superior to our own may also be able to sense changes in barometric pressure? If they can, then perhaps, like geese, the rate of pressure change could trigger certain instinctive behavior. Years of field observation have led me to believe this is indeed the case, and we'll focus on just what those behaviors are a bit later on. We still have some ground to cover in our basic understanding of weather.

In the vast sea of air that surrounds us, there is a constant effort underway to equal things out. Air always flows from areas of high atmospheric pressure into areas of low atmospheric pressure. A large blue "H" depicts centers of high-pressure areas on weather maps. A large red "L" depicts centers of low-pressure systems. Wind flow around high-pressure areas in our part of the world is clockwise, out and away from the center. Wind flow around low-pressure systems is counterclockwise and into the center. On weather maps, lines are often drawn connecting points of equal barometric pressure called isobars and serve the same purpose as lines connecting equal elevation on a topographic map by helping meteorologists get a 3-D picture of the atmosphere over a given region.

Just as tightly packed lines on a topographic map show hunters the steepness of the slope of the land, so too the isobars show the meteorologist the "slope" between the centers of high and low pressure. If you were to empty the contents of a water container on a steep slope, you'd expect the water to flow downhill more rapidly than it would on a gradual slope. In the same way, air moves faster "downhill" from the high to the low the more tightly packed the isobars are and the result is higher surface winds. The only difference is that, unlike the water on the hill example, there is something called the Coriolis effect that causes air not to flow directly across the isobars from the high to the low, but to do so at an angle. On the day pictured in the weather map on page 23 there were strong winds from the east in eastern Colorado and from the northeast across western Nebraska. I don't want to get too deep here, other than to say the Coriolis effect is what's behind the way winds turn as air moves from high to low pressure. What's this got to do with hunting deer? Plenty. Being aware of what the wind will do through the course of a day when the atmosphere is in transition at your hunting ground will help you plan your stalk, use and control your scents most effectively, and tell you where you don't want to be in order to prevent being winded by your quarry.

Weather fronts are characterized by the air masses that drive them forward, and it helps greatly to think three-

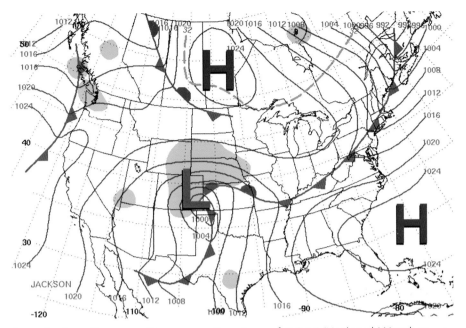

A typical surface weather map. Courtesy of NOAA/National Weather Service. Public domain.

dimensionally when discussing them. Dr. Michael Pidwirny of the University of British Columbia, Okanagan, has a superb and easy-to-understand Internet page devoted to the discussion of interacting air masses and fronts that you can visit at http://www.physicalgeography.net/fundamentals/7r.html, and he graciously allowed me to share some of the information and graphics from his website with you here.

Cold fronts appear on weather maps as blue lines with triangles, also known as barbs, pointing in the direction of the front's movement. They mark the leading edge of colder, drier air pushing into warmer, moister air. Cold air is denser than warm air, and cold fronts move faster than warm fronts. If you took a cross-section of the atmosphere looking along a line perpendicular to a cold front's movement and could visually see what was happening it would look a lot like the image pictured on page 24.

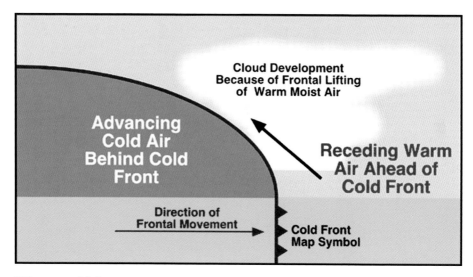

What a cold front would look like from the side if we were capable of visualizing colliding air masses. Graphic courtesy of Dr. Michael Pidwirny of the University of British Columbia, Okanagan. Used by permission.

Cold air sinks, and warm air rises. The cold front has a "snowplow effect" on the warm air ahead of it, forcing the warm and moister air upward. Because warm air holds more moisture than cold air, and air cools as it rises, a strong cold front will tend to wring the moisture out of the air it displaces upward resulting in brief, but sometimes very heavy precipitation.

Anyone who has been outside when a cold front moves through can see and feel the signs of the front's passage readily. There is usually a sudden change in wind direction from south or southeast to north or northwest, and the temperature falls rapidly. Thunderstorms, sleet or snow squalls can be present. Barometric pressure rises rapidly, and the passage of cold fronts during fall hunting seasons will often be accompanied by very gusty winds. Every big-game hunter should take extra precautions and gear if a hunt is planned on a day that a cold front is predicted to cross the area. I've seen weather go from low 50s and calm to 20s with howling wind and low-visibility in snow, all in about an hour's time. If I hadn't planned ahead by bringing my waterproof and windproof camo, insulated boots, gloves and an extra layer of clothing I might have been at risk of hypothermia. Getting caught unexpectedly by the sudden onset of cold weather and precipitation is one of the most common ways hunters find themselves in trouble. We'll talk more about how animals react to cold fronts later, but for now just remember what they can do to you.

Warm fronts are shown on weather maps as red lines with red half circles showing the direction of movement. They advance much more slowly than cold fronts and mark the area where warm and moist air is moving across and displacing cool, dry air.

As you can see from the image pictured on the following page, if a cold front compares to a snowplow, a warm front is more like a broom. In the vicinity of an advancing warm front, the temperature actually increases with altitude until the front has passed. High cirrostratus clouds will often precede a warm front by hundreds of miles with the cloud deck getting progressively lower as the front gets closer. Because of the way the warm air layer drags itself over the top of the cold air, it is the kind of situation where precipitation can begin in liquid form aloft. It then either freezes into ice pellets as it falls through the cold-air layer near the ground or actually freezes on contact with cold objects at the surface as freezing rain or freezing drizzle, if the surface temperature is sufficiently below freezing. Precipitation associated with a warm front is usually longer in duration than precipitation with a cold front, so you

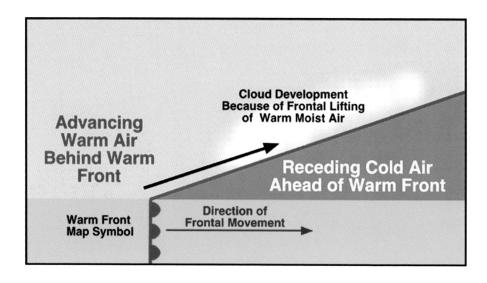

Advancing
Warm Air
Behind Warm
Front

Cloud Development
Because of Frontal Lifting
of Warm Moist Air

Receding Cold Air
Ahead of Warm Front

Warm Front
Map Symbol

Direction of
Frontal Movement

What a warm front would look like from the side if we were capable of visualizing colliding air masses. Graphic courtesy of Dr. Michael Pidwirny of the University of British Columbia, Okanagan. Used by permission.

can't count on the old saying, "Rain before seven is done by eleven," though it will usually subside once the warm front has passed. Warm fronts are a good news/bad news event for hunters. The good news is that hunters wanting a break from hunting in frigid conditions will get it. The bad news is that the transition to warmer weather can mean extended periods of foul weather. And, as we'll soon see, when a warm front comes through there usually is a cold front not far behind.

Cold fronts move faster than warm fronts and will eventually overtake them. The part of a low-pressure storm system where this happens is called an occlusion and marked on maps by an occluded front.

Occluded fronts are depicted either as purple or as alternating red and blue

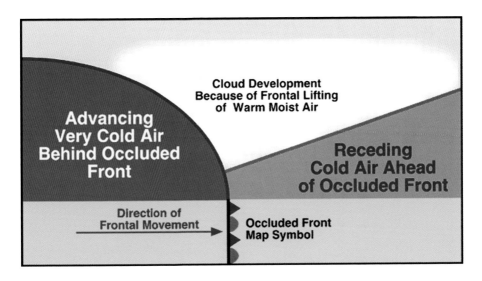

Cloud Development Because of Frontal Lifting of Warm Moist Air

Advancing Very Cold Air Behind Occluded Front

Receding Cold Air Ahead of Occluded Front

Direction of Frontal Movement →

Occluded Front Map Symbol

segments with bumps and barbs facing the same direction and exhibit properties of both warm and cold fronts to some extent. They tend to bring the prolonged precipitation of the warm front with a reinforcing shot of even colder air. To keep it simple, let's just say hunters should associate occluded fronts with prolonged periods of foul weather and either be equipped to deal with it or plan on playing a lot of poker at the lodge or camp.

A stationary front is, as the name implies, a boundary between two distinct air masses not going anywhere. It is shown on weather maps as alternating red and blue segments with bumps and barbs facing opposite directions. The surface weather map shown on page 28 depicts a stationary front stretching east across central Canada, and another from Alabama into

What an occluded front would look like from the side if we were capable of visualizing colliding air masses. Graphic courtesy of Dr. Michael Pidwirny of the University of British Columbia, Okanagan. Used by permission.

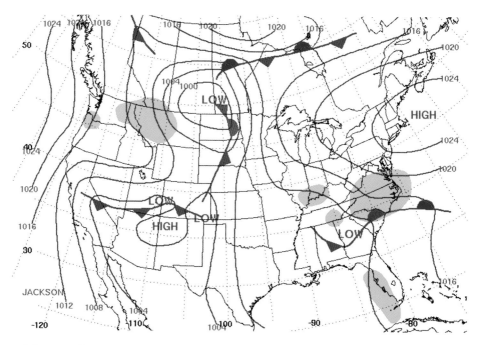

This weather map shows stationary fronts extending from Alabama to South Carolina and from Manitoba to Quebec. An occluded front is pictured across eastern North Dakota. Photo courtesy of the National Weather Service. Public Domain.

South Carolina. Drastic weather conditions are seldom associated with stationary fronts, but sometimes upper-level disturbances or small low-pressure centers can track along them and trigger showers or thunderstorms that are generally short in duration. Make sure you don't confuse stationary fronts with the alternating blue and red segments of an occluded front where bumps and barbs appear on the same side.

Occasionally, you'll see a bold dashed line on a weather map. That depicts a low-pressure trough. These transitory and often elongated areas are like ditches of low pressure in the atmosphere and can trigger brief periods of precipitation and cloud cover as they move through, along with a shift in wind direction.

Dave Ranard, President and CEO of Creative Outdoor Products, Inc., the company that developed the Hunter Dan line of products for children, arrowed this huge buck on a cloudless "bluebird day" in Indiana during the opening day of the 2005 bow season. Big bucks can be taken in almost any kind of weather. The key to success is understanding how weather can work to your advantage. Photo used by permission.

We've covered a lot of basic weather information in this section, and I hope you've found it both interesting and helpful. But now it's time to get to the meat of the matter, pun intended, and show how various weather situations influence the behavior of deer and other game animals. Not only that, I'll show you how to adapt your hunting tactics to the weather at your hunting ground and use the weather to up your chances of filling your tag.

CHAPTER 2

Hunting Under Pressure

Given the highly active nature of North America's weather, seldom does barometric pressure remain relatively steady for days at a time during hunting seasons. One exception to this would be for areas established under a large upper-level ridge as shown by an inverted "U" on a map of the jet stream. That pattern, also known as an "omega block" for its resemblance to that letter of the Greek alphabet, is characterized by hot, dry weather lasting many days or even a few weeks. But in North America, the omega block is largely a summertime pattern. During spring turkey or bear and fall big-game seasons you can count on changing atmospheric pressure. The change in barometric pressure serves to indicate what kind of weather is on the way, and how game is likely to respond. As the title of this book indicates, I'll be focusing on the relationship between various elements of weather and deer. Many of my findings, however, will also aid hunters of other big-game species such as elk and antelope.

I've been hunting and observing deer on the same piece of ground in western South Dakota for nearly 15 years, and one of the many observations I've made is that

This Texas whitetail was out making his rounds as barometric pressure fell in advance of an approaching weather system. Photo by David Downs. Used by permission.

deer activity level and behavior changes do coincide with changes in barometric pressure. When the atmospheric pressure is falling, the deer get active and the faster the pressure drops the more active the deer are. The increase in activity manifests itself primarily in a deer herd's feeding patterns, but also in mating behavior if the rut is on. Atmospheric pressure will decrease preceding the passage of both warm and cold fronts. Deer can be hunted successfully no matter what the barometer is doing, but my observations lead me to conclude that deer become especially active in situations where the barometric pressure is sharply dropping ahead of an approaching strong cold front or low-pressure system, and the more deer that are on the move, the more opportunities for hunters to encounter them.

A healthy whitetail deer will consume about 10 pounds of food each day usually divided into an early morning and late afternoon feeding cycle. I've observed the afternoon feeding session to be the more lengthy of the two with a pronounced increase in deer movement about two hours prior to the onset of darkness and peaking during the last hour of light. This information is nothing new to veteran hunters, but the feeding schedule may be altered considerably during periods of significant changes in barometric pressure.

Pressure changes become greater as a front gets closer. Deer sense significant change in weather and will feed right up to the moment of frontal passage. They will then seek the shelter of trees, shelterbelts, standing crops, creek bottoms and ditches. If a changing pressure tells deer to expect a major weather change during the course of a day, say mid-morning, I've seen them extend the morning feeding period as they fill up with as much forage as possible before heading for shelter. While I won't speculate as to the degree of intelligence deer possess pertaining to matters of meteorological science, it seems as if they know ahead of time that weather could prevent their usual afternoon feeding. Thus they eat as much food as possible beforehand.

This group of three nice Texas whitetail bucks and a spike were eager to eat their fill. The next day a weather system moved in with rain and thunderstorms. Photo by David Downs. Used by permission.

These days there are a number of tools available to hunters for detecting changes in barometric pressure. Sure, that old reliable wall barometer on the hunting lodge wall may be both effective and traditional, but barometric pressure tendencies can now also be monitored on GPS units, portable handheld weather stations and even some watches. By barometric pressure tendency I mean showing how much atmospheric pressure has changed over a specified time period, usually between three and 12 hours. Barometric pressure can be measured in inches of mercury, bars, Pascals, millimeters of mercury or atmospheres, but don't let all this confuse you. No matter what unit a barometer measures pressure in, what hunters really need to know is the pressure tendency (rising or falling) and rate of change. I've been using a portable handheld Kestrel weather station since my

Perhaps old fashioned, but still reliable and affordable, wall-mounted barometer/ thermometer units can come in handy at home or at the hunting lodge before a hunt. Photo by author.

A Compact, handheld weather instrument can be a valuable tool for hunters. The Kestrel 4000 is one of several units on the market that display atmospheric pressure, pressure change over time and altitude information.
Photo by author.

days as a consultant meteorologist, and I also saw several of my former wildland firefighter colleagues use similar units.

There are even wristwatches available at reasonable prices that are equipped with altimeters and built-in barometers that display pressure tendency, altitude and navigation information.

The Summit Highgear Watch displays both current barometric pressure (yellow box in millibars) and pressure tendency over the most recent 24 hours in the form of a graph (blue box shows falling pressure, then a slight rise to stable pressure with partly cloudy skies – an indication of frontal passage). Photo by author.

Barometric pressure was dropping on the evening this photo was taken at a stagnant pond, and bubbles could occasionally be seen rising up from the bottom. Photo by author.

Nature will also provide hunters with clues that the barometric pressure is falling when hi-tech gadgets aren't available. Watch the altitude at which passing flocks of migratory birds fly. They'll tend to fly closer to the ground when low pressure is moving in. Flying insects will also buzz around and swarm closer to the ground when air pressure is dropping. I've mentioned large mammals becoming more active when the pressure heads downward, but small animals also seem to increase their activity when pressure drops. You may see more activity from rabbits, squirrels, mice and predators that feed on them such as coyotes and foxes. The characteristic stench of decay hunters often encounter around marshes and swamps will increase as lower pressure exerted on that small ecosystem allows gasses held underwater by high atmospheric pressure to bubble to the surface and be released into the air.

If the water is deep enough to hold fish, you might notice an increase in surface feeding as tiny organisms bubble up to the surface with the aforementioned gasses and create an abundance of food for the fish that feed on them. And don't forget that aches and pains from old injuries will flair up when barometric pressure falls rapidly. So once a hunter determines that pressure is dropping and will continue to do so, what tactics should be most likely to result in success?

Deer aren't the only animals that feed aggressively when weather changes are on the way. This javelina was part of a group of the animals that threw caution to the wind to get a few nibbles of corn the day before the weather turned foul on a south Texas ranch. They didn't care that the author was a mere 10-yards away with an H.S. Precision .30-06. Big-game animals, predators, birds, small animals, fish and insects all become more active when barometric pressure falls in advance of a storm.

First of all, it's important to remember not to strategize based on a single weather variable. Along will falling barometric pressure, there will be other weather parameters at work that might require a tactical adjustment. As pressure drops with an approaching front, there will likely be increasing cloud cover, a prevailing wind direction, precipitation moving in and so forth. But the deer will be doing three things when the pressure tendency is consistently downward. They'll be moving, they'll be eating more and for longer periods of time, and when the front finally moves in along with the accompanying change in wind direction, onset of precipitation and increasing wind velocity, the deer will be moving to cover.

Major storm systems moving across North America can start the barometric pressure trend heading downward 24-36 hours or more ahead of frontal passage. If I know I've got a day or more before the weather turns, I'll spend day one of my hunt in an ambush position with a clear view of a known feeding area all day. I don't hunt from treestands as a matter of personal preference, and even my bowhunting is spot-and-stalk from ground level, so I'll head to the edge of a creek bed or drop into a depression in the ground where I can observe the most area possible while remaining relatively invisible.

Familiarity with the terrain you'll be hunting is essential, right down to the last yard of elevation. Such knowledge is best obtained by preseason scouting, but this isn't always possible when hunting areas you've never seen before. That's where meticulous study of topographic maps and satellite photos becomes essential. Once you've obtained such familiarity, consider setting up a portable blind, get into your treestand, or make yourself as comfortably concealed as possible below the lip of a creek bed, in a dry

Familiarity with the terrain in the area you'll be hunting is critical. Detailed topographic maps, satellite images and conversation with those who have experience in the area can be most helpful. Photo by author.

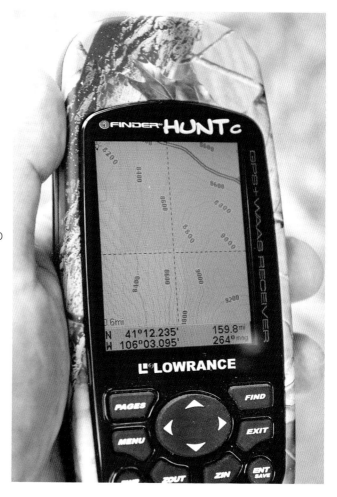

ditch or concealed by trees and brush where as much of the feeding ground as possible can be seen. Wind direction when pressure is dropping ahead of an approaching cold front will be from the south to southeast in most cases, so put yourself on the north to west side of the feeding area if possible.

The day before a storm or front arrives and serious feeding begins, I've often seen deer engaging in social behavior in middle of the day during times when they are usually bedded down. I've noticed this more with whitetails than mule deer, but it stands in stark contrast to

days when atmospheric pressure is rising. I've seen more buck movement in particular, including sparring matches between bucks, on days before bad weather moves in than at any other time in the field. If the rut is on, the bucks seem more energized by a sense of urgency to "complete the mission" before full attention may have to be devoted to surviving a coming storm and its aftermath. On such days, pack your lunch with you and have everything you'll need on hand for a full day of hunting. Plan to hunt from a half hour before sunrise until the conclusion of legal shooting hours, and whatever you do, don't make the mistake of heading back to the lodge, camp or town in the middle of the day. You may miss out on a great opportunity to fill your tag in rather nice weather before the approaching storm arrives.

This whitetail buck took advantage of good weather before an approaching storm arrived. Photo courtesy of the Black Hills Pioneer Newspaper.

There has been speculation by some that falling barometric pressure "triggers" rut activity in bucks of breeding age. Personally, I have not seen sufficient evidence to support that conclusion. I attribute any increase in rut-related deer behavior just prior to a front's arrival as having more to do with opportunity than air pressure. Since deer and other animals generally become more active as barometric pressure drops prior to frontal passage, it's logical to conclude that a love-starved buck will encounter more deer moving through his area and the result will be more rubbing, scraping, skirmishing and mating.

Make sure you pay close attention to weather reports on the day the front is supposed to move through. Monitor NOAA weather radio frequencies to try and get as close a fix as possible on the exact time the front will be moving through your hunting ground and start the barometric pressure rising. Keep in mind that the passage of any front will bring rising pressure and a change in wind direction.

You'll want to position yourself downwind of the areas you know are holding deer initially, but you'll have to be mobile during that critical hour before the front passes to avoid being scented as the wind direction changes. If landowner considerations, safety factors, good sportsman conduct or other aspects of your situation require that you pick a spot and stay there all day when you know the winds will be changing from southeast to northwest, try to take up a position northeast of where you expect that the deer will be active if the low pressure area is to your north. However, you'll need to take up a position southwest of the deer if the low-pressure center is to your south. These are the least likely directions from which wind will blow toward the deer, depending on where the low-pressure center is. When low

Paying close attention to the wind direction, good camo and using terrain to your advantage is key to success in any big-game hunt. A steady easterly wind and a milky-colored layer of stratus clouds told the author that low pressure was south of his location during a 2006 bison hunt. A painstaking stalk from the southwest put him and his guide within 40 yards of this meat bull when the animal was felled by a single shot from the .470 Nitro Express the author was field-testing for Cabela's.

pressure passes to the north during the day, southeast winds will gradually become, south, then southwest and then west to northwest. If the low-pressure center passes to your south, easterly winds will become northeast, then north and finally northwest. So how can a hunter figure out where the low-pressure center is if there's no access to a weather map?

Remember that air always flows from high-pressure areas outward and downward in a clockwise direction into low-pressure centers spinning counterclockwise where it is lifted upward. In 1857, a Dutch meteorologist named Christoph Heinrich Diedrich Buys Ballot came up with what we know today as the Buys Ballot Law. It states that, in the Northern Hemisphere at mid-latitudes (that would be much of the U.S. and Europe) if you stand with your back to the wind, the low-pressure center will be to your left. In a hunting application, if you notice as you leave your vehicle for your blind or stand that the wind is blowing out of the south, the lower barometric pressure is to your west. If the wind is out of the east, lower barometric pressure is to your south. Watching for changes in wind direction throughout the day will keep you abreast of where a low-pressure center is located relative to your position and help you predict what further changes in the wind might take place in coming hours. This, in turn, will aid you in deploying scents and attractants to your advantage while avoiding positioning yourself where game could get a whiff of you and run off.

The sharply angled smoke column from this farmer's burn pile was a sign of lowering barometric pressure. I watched the smoke for about 30 minutes before taking this picture to ensure the bent column wasn't a localized anomaly, and then snapped the shot just as it started to rain. Photo by author.

Scent-control clothing can reduce your risk of being winded, but you'll want a moisture-wicking layer next to your skin to keep perspiration from wetting your inner layer as you move about during the day. I'm a big fan of the newer antimicrobial moisture-wicking layers impregnated with silver threads. These threads use silver's special properties to neutralize human odors before they can form. A moisture-wicking inner layer next to your skin will also keep you from becoming cold if the approaching front is a strong cold front with a sharp temperature drop. We'll look a fronts a bit more closely later, but we still have some important things to consider pertaining to high- and low-pressure hunting situations.

One old weather proverb that has stood the test of time and appeared in various forms has to do with using campfire smoke to predict weather. Smoke will rise vertically, almost straight up in an area under the influence of high pressure. That means the next day's weather is likely to be fair. Horizontal movement of campfire smoke means the pressure is falling and a change is likely on the way. All of this assumes, of course, relatively calm conditions around the campfire, but should start your mind plotting strategy concerning the use of scents and attractants (where legal). Reviewing the weather forecast before you head out to your treestand will tell you what the expected prevailing winds will be as you hunt through the day, and scent-producing lure products that use a lighter-than-air dispersal method will disperse the product in a fashion similar to that of the smoke you saw coming off the morning campfire or out of the camp stove chimney. Use of scent and attractant lures can be very effective when the barometer is falling because the lowest levels of the atmosphere tend to be more humid as low-level moisture is transported by prevailing winds toward the center of low pressure. But that doesn't mean you should leave the Tink's or Buck Bomb at home if the barometer is rising.

Rising barometric pressure is associated with cooler and often drier air moving into a region. Air under high pressure sinks, a process meteorologists call subsidence. Initially the cold front ushering in higher pressure is likely to bring

This whitetail buck was harvested by the author on a cloudless day with calm winds after a high-pressure area established itself over the hunting ground following the passage of a front a couple of days earlier. More than two-dozen deer were seen that morning engaged in aggressive feeding, and this rutting buck had just finished a joust with a smaller one before running headlong into the hunter's ambush position in tall grass overlooking a field.

gusty winds that will disperse scent products intended to lure deer so rapidly that you're better off saving your money and not using them at all. But once winds die down 12-24 hours after the front moves through, high pressure induces very calm and still conditions along with sinking air. This will keep deer-luring scent products trapped near the ground, especially if a low-level temperature inversion is in place. If you see ground fog or low-hanging mists over the marshes that are slow to lift or disperse, use your scent lures generously because they'll remain effective even long after the morning fog or mist has lifted. The air is still sinking slowly around your stand or blind, and the moisture you saw close to the ground is painting every tree trunk, leaf or blade of grass with that scent.

While I've witnessed very aggressive feeding by whitetail deer when the barometric pressure is falling, I have also seen deer feed with gusto after the atmospheric turmoil that often accompanies a front ushering in high pressure subsides. Deer that have been hunkered down in the blustery conditions that accompany a frontal passage that sets the barometer rising like a balloon will come out to replenish their energy resources as the rise in pressure stabilizes into a more gradual ascent. The first calm morning following the passage of a front that came in with lots of wind and rapidly rising pressure can be as productive for hunting as the period of falling pressure that preceded the front.

During fall and winter hunts, high-pressure is often associated with very cold weather conditions. Because the air molecules under an area of dense high atmospheric pressure are more closely packed together, sound waves are propagated more efficiently. In other words, sounds seem louder and travel farther and that means hunters must take extra care to exercise stealth during every move made. Perhaps you've noticed how sounds such as aircraft flying overhead, the crunching of snow or frozen leaves underfoot, and even racking a round from the magazine of your rifle into the chamber seem to be amplified by cold high pressure. Because cold air holds less moisture than warm air, the likelihood of encountering significant precipitation when cold high pressure dominates your hunting ground is minimal. In such conditions, insulated fleece, wool or new silent synthetic blends would be the best choice for an outer layer because they are inherently quiet. Be certain all of your gear items, including ammo, binoculars, rangefinders GPS units and the like are secured in your pack or on your person in a way so that they don't rattle or click together when you walk. This is a good practice to get into regardless of the air pressure, but remember that game may be able to hear you farther away when the pressure is high and the temperature is well below freezing.

Conversely, warm air holds more moisture than cold air and warm, moist conditions are often associated with low pressure moving into an area. Because the air molecules are spaced farther apart in areas of falling barometric pressure, sound doesn't travel as far and is also perceived not to be as loud. But any sound-deadening advantages associated with falling pressure may be negated by an increase in humidity, as moisture is an excellent sound transmission medium. In some parts of the United States, however, fronts and low-pressure troughs can move through areas without much increase in humidity. Such conditions are quite common from southwestern desert areas eastward into west Texas. Sounds will not seem as loud or travel as

far in warm weather with low pressure and low to moderate humidity as they will in cold weather with high pressure.

As a general rule of thumb, deer hunters are likely to encounter more deer when the barometric pressure is falling, but don't let a rising barometer stop you from heading out after that trophy buck. When the atmospheric violence that often accompanies a transition from low- to high-pressure dominance over an area subsides, deer that have been waiting out the storm will come out in droves seeking food. Remember that barometric pressure rises rapidly in the wake of a strong cold front, and strong cold fronts mean strong winds. As we'll soon see, that post-frontal period of windy weather can be the spot-and-stalk hunter's ally.

CHAPTER 3

Hunting on the Front Lines

It was one of those situations many big-game hunters find themselves in at one time or another. I had a deer tag to fill, and due to work obligations I had only one afternoon to hunt before the season would end. No matter what the weather was going to do, I decided days in advance that the hunt would go on.

My license was for a muzzleloader season in an area where only antlerless deer could be harvested, and I'd anticipated having a pretty good chance to fill my tag because the private land I was hunting had too many whitetails feeding on the landowner's haystacks at night. I started monitoring the weather closely as the day of the hunt drew near and realized I'd be facing a significant weather challenge. A powerful Canadian cold front was going to be crossing my hunting ground, and it looked like I had little chance of beating it. I was right, and I didn't.

The cold front had moved through about an hour before I got to the farm. I hunkered down behind some hay bales and started glassing the land. Winds were blowing from the northwest at sustained speeds up to 30 mph with gusts in the 40-50 mph range. I could feel the temperature falling as I stood there, and I expected that wind chill factors would be nearing zero before long. I'd hunted that land for more than a dozen years, and I had timed my mid-afternoon arrival to coincide with the time I would usually see the deer coming out of the tree line and into the field before me. But I knew there would be no deer moving that afternoon. They were bedded down somewhere, riding out the howling wind in shelter.

Knowledge of the land you are going to hunt is vital. Its importance cannot be over emphasized. In the 12 or so years I'd spent hunting with rifles, bows and muzzleloaders on that piece of ground I knew exactly where I would find deer. Smack dab in the middle of the property is a ridge about 25 feet higher than the land below it. The ridge runs northwest to southeast a short distance before curving due south about 300 yards and then turning due east to create an elongated "S" shape. At the base of that ridge is a boggy area covered in cattails about 100 yards wide and 200 yards long. That would be target area number one.

The northwest winds that blow in behind a strong cold front blow pretty straight and strong for at least a few hours after frontal passage. In other words, you don't have to worry about them shifting much on you. I went due south from my truck about a quarter mile into the farm field until the center point of the ridge overlooking the cattails was due east of me about 200 yards. In that position, the northwest winds would be carrying my scent across the southernmost section of the cattails, an area where the cover was thinnest. I then stalked to the top edge of the slope, covering the last yards close to the ground with the sun right at my back.

Hunters are always justifiably concerned about having their human silhouette "skylined" by high ground, but I've learned that deer don't like to stare directly into the sun any more than you or I do, so in the early morning and late afternoon I use that fact to my advantage whenever possible. I already knew what was going to happen anyway. I was going to rise to full height with my Optima muzzleloader at the ready, let my very long shadow fall across the cattails, and slowly walk the edge of the ridge until the deer I knew were hiding in the thick stuff stood up and presented me with a shot. The shadow would get their attention, the northwest wind wouldn't let them catch my scent, the sun would blind them when they looked in my direction, and I'd drop the first deer that stood and tried to sort things out. That's exactly the way things happened, except for one little detail. A deer did stand up right where I thought it would, and I brought up the Optima quickly, lining up the sights on the animal's shoulder just 30 yards away. Then I lowered my muzzleloader. It was a dandy, full-bodied whitetail buck. My tag was for an antlerless deer and this one had a 4 x 4 rack. The buck bolted when I lowered my gun, but suddenly there was a flurry of movement out of the corner of my eye to my right. A doe and a couple of fawns were running full speed out of the south edge of the cattails 100-yards away. The three deer accelerated when their path intersected the wind direction and their nostrils got a full dose of me. I won't take running shots at that range with a smokepole of any kind, and I don't shoot does with offspring as a matter of personal preference. They gave me the slip while I was admiring the buck, and I watched them disappear over the rise. So much for plan A. It was time for plan B, and I had no plan C as the sun was sinking lower, the wind was getting stronger and my toes and fingers were telling me it was time to get a move on.

There's a river, more of a creek actually, that marks the north and east boundaries of the land I hunt. Beneath the canopy of old and wide hardwoods that line the creek is a shorter area of dense brush behind which is a flat grassy area between the brush and bank. The brush and sun hid me from view as I slipped down into the creek bottom due south of my objective. The gusty northwest wind now blew against the left side of my face and I felt it burn my

When cold and blustery winds rush in behind a cold front, a slow walk through heavy cover such as cattails or thick grass can often be productive. Photo by author.

Using the weather conditions to his advantage allowed the author to fill his antlerless tag with the .50-caliber CVA Optima muzzleloader pictured in about a half hour. Photo by author.

cheek as I angled to stalk due north very slowly. In a very short time I saw the telltale sign of deer ears in the grass between the creek and brush in an area sheltered from the wind. I let my camo do its job and used the roar of the wind rustling through the brush and branches to my advantage. The two bedded whitetails were unable to see, hear or smell me as I closed the distance to 30 ft. I raised my Optima into shooting position, cocked it, remained motionless, and then grunted loud enough to be heard over the wind. Both deer stood, and the more curious of the two actually took a few steps toward me. With my muzzleloader already aimed and ready, there was nothing left to do but pull the trigger. The 245-grain PowerBelt AeroTip entered dead center of the throat and obliterated the offside neck vertebrae of the young deer 25-feet away. It dropped where it had stood without so much as a twitch. Sheltered by the brush, I tagged and field-dressed the antlerless deer and phoned a colleague at work to tell him the news. Dramatically dropping temperatures, a skyrocketing barometer and a bitter howling wind that blew dirt and grit from area fields you could feel on your

Every hunter must be certain where his or her bullet will go after the shot. This mule deer buck is standing on the edge of a rise, beneath which is a road that runs about a quarter mile downrange through the trees. Photo by Dave Downs. Used by permission.

front teeth had not prevented me from filling my tag in less than 30 minutes. Why? I knew the lay of the land precisely, had a pretty good idea where deer would be sheltering with a northwest wind that strong, used the blinding sun and wind noise to mask my approach and let the weather generated by the recent passage of a cold front help me fill my tag instead of hinder me.

My good fortune that day lay in the fact that the cold front, though very strong, had little atmospheric moisture to work with to produce precipitation. Had the front produced significant snow, I would have had to decide if I should proceed with the hunt or not. Wind-driven snow would not have altered my tactics and would have forced deer to look into the snow to try to see me, something they don't like to do because the snow gets in their eyes and ears. To that extent a snow squall would have aided me. Snow squalls tend to be short-lived, but sometimes intense periods of snow that accompany the passage of a cold front that is strong, but not part of a major snow-producing winter storm system. There are two reasons I might have had to decide to stop my hunt if it had been snowing, and both have to do with safety.

It is the responsibility of every hunter to know where his or her bullet will end its flight. I cannot tell you how many times I've heard the unnerving whizzing sound of a bullet whip past me or the even more frightening "whiz-THWAP" as a bullet hit the ground, a tree or a fencepost next to me. In each such case a hunter shooting at a skylined animal between my position and his fired the shot or he simply "didn't see me," an excuse I find incomprehensible given my resemblance to a giant pumpkin when hunting during seasons that require the use of blaze orange.

Fog can mess with a hunter's vision and mind. Take a hard look at this photo. What exactly do you think you see? Are the dark areas islands on a lake or clumps of marsh in a slough? How far away are they? Is the picture upside down? Can you find the deer in the picture? Are there deer in the picture? I think you can see why a shot in this area at this time wouldn't be safe. Photo by Craig Goodrich.

Hunting in snow, fog, heavy drizzle or other visibility-reducing precipitation can obscure a hunter's view of the area behind his or her target for a considerable distance. Because I hunt in cattle ranch country, I want to be certain there isn't a steer, tractor or horse downrange hidden by precipitation. If visibility is a quarter mile in falling and blowing snow, you may be able to get close to a deer for a shot, but if you miss, your bullet could still travel another few miles. If you can't see what's beyond the deer and don't have a good natural backstop you shouldn't be shooting.

The other safety factor has to do with retrieval, travel and hypothermia. Snow is slippery. The place where my deer fell was about 900 yards from my truck. I'm in my mid-40s and of hefty build. Because the cold front that swept through my area that afternoon was dry, the dirt on the ground between my truck and me was already freezing and hardening from the cold by the time my field-dressing work was done. Moisture on the gut pile and my knife was turning to ice. It was a chilly, but relatively easy walk back to the truck. Had there been a couple of inches of snow on the ground however, the conditions on that field would have been slick, and my hike back into the wind more strenuous. If I hadn't had a moisture-wicking base layer I could have become very cold. In a worst case scenario I could have lost sight of where I was going in blowing snow and started becoming hypothermic and disoriented. Then I'd have had to risk the truck getting stuck in the field on the way to and from the downed deer, and a hazardous drive back home.

Hunting in any weather demands stealth. Spotting game before it spots you is critical to success. Texas hog hunter, Craig Goodrich, put out a trail of corn to attract boars. He took this photo as he waited in ambush. Both the buck and the bunnies in the foreground were oblivious to his presence. Used by permission.

I've hunted in snow many times and will talk about that more in the section of this book that deals with hunting in various kinds of precipitation, but for me the dangers of hunting in significant blowing snow extend beyond my personal safety limits. Those are a few things to keep in mind when a strong cold front brings snow squalls with it.

When cold fronts do bring precipitation in the spring and early fall, it tends to be shorter in duration than that generated by warm fronts and occluded fronts but can still be quite intense. Usually the strength of the front as determined by the contrast in air masses ahead of it and behind it will give you a clue as to how long deer will be riding the weather out in sheltered areas. If you're watching weather forecasts for your hunting area and hear that high temperatures one day will be in the 50s but only in the 20s the next day, that's a pretty strong front. The stronger the front, usually the longer the period of high winds associated with it's passage and the greater the likelihood of significant precipitation if there is sufficient atmospheric moisture for the front to work with.

After I weigh the safety element involved in hunting around a cold front, I'll adjust my tactics accordingly. I find the most effective way to hunt deer from the time the cold front hits and 12- to 24-hours afterwards is to spot-and-stalk through cover. You won't find me in a blind when it's windy, and because deer won't be moving much the odds of success still hunting or hunting from ground blinds and elevated stands are diminished. When it comes to windy cold front hunting, I don't wait for the deer to come to me. I go to them.

There are four key components to deer hunting success in cover, at ground level, in the windy conditions generated

Deer have excellent vision, and this bug-eyed buck apparently saw something he didn't like when Zach Even's trail camera snapped his picture from a western Nebraska tree trunk. Photo courtesy of Zach Even.

by a cold front's passage. Those are keen eyesight, very slow and quiet movement, knowledge of the land you hunt and remembering to always keep areas you think may hold deer upwind of your position.

First, it is vital that you see the deer before it sees you. Some may wonder how that's possible for hunters clad head to toe in blaze orange during seasons that require it, and that's a fair question. Whenever possible and legal during seasons when blaze orange must be worn, I wear blaze camo. I recommend blaze camo with a soft and quiet shell material and a breathable waterproof membrane inside to

In states and regions where it meets legal requirements, the author recommends the use of blaze orange camo outerwear and believes it does help break up the human outline to some extent.

let perspiration vapor escape. Incorporating scent control into such a garment is always beneficial, but remember you're keeping the promising areas upwind so it's not as critical in this kind of hunting situation. I'm not a deer biologist so I can't comment on the validity of claims about the effectiveness of blaze camo from the perspective of an expert on deer eyesight, but I do know from personal experience that deer have apparently had a tough time seeing me if I'm still when wearing it.

Hunters know deer are keenly tuned to watch for movement with eye placement on the sides of their heads that affords more than 300 degrees of visibility, and the wonderful thing about hunting after a strong front has passed is that everything in the deer's environment is blown about by the wind. Everywhere a deer looks it sees movement. Trees, branches, bushes, crops and grass are all swaying as the colder, denser air pours in. The noise of strong wind blowing through cover is loud enough to hunters, but for a deer relying on hearing as a primary defense mechanism it must be deafening and very confusing. The hours after a strong cold front passes really mess with two key deer defenses, those being eyesight and hearing, and that's what makes hunting in such conditions highly desirable for closing to shooting distance.

This ties in with the second key component to success when hunting in the windiest hours after frontal passage: slow and quiet movement. Wear whatever you legally can to break up your outline and quiet your movements as you tread slowly and carefully so the deer will have far greater difficulty hearing you and seeing you. I've often discovered that deer bedded in cover after a windy frontal passage are agitated and nervous. Their ears flick this way and that

Be patient when hunting in cover. Wait for the deer to expose his vitals for the sure-kill shot. Hunting in cover is hard work and I've seen many hunters complete a good stalk only to rush the shot and miss. Reward your work with patience and opportunity will present itself.

trying to isolate sounds that constitute a threat from those that are just wind generated, and their heads are constantly turning to verify or dismiss the presence of danger. If you're moving very slowly into the wind you have a good chance of spotting the deer before they spot you because of their quick head and ear movements. While use of binoculars is often associated with open-country hunting, I use mine hunting in cover too. On more than one occasion my use of optics has enabled me to locate deer bedded in cover less than 100-yards away and helped me avoid detection. Once you've located the deer and they remain oblivious to your presence, the final components for cold-front hunting success come into play.

Hunting deer in cover is always challenging because of the need to have a clear shot. There is really no such thing as a "brush busting" caliber, and that means moving into a shooting position where you can see the target animal's vitals clearly without being detected. Familiarity with the land you hunt will come in very handy in such a situation. There have been times when I've had to backtrack a considerable distance after locating deer in cover so that I could take advantage of a brush line, ditch or creek bed and start a new upwind approach. This takes time and patience, but is well worth it. It's very gratifying to defeat a deer's natural defenses to such an extent as to be able to stalk to within 10 feet or less, as I have done on more than one occasion. But remember what is required in order to do so. See the deer first, move very slowly and quietly, use the terrain and cover present to your advantage and stay downwind of the deer on approach. These tactics have proven themselves time and again during the windy hours after a cold front has moved through and deer are waiting it out in shelter.

A winter day dawns over Rapid City, South Dakota with a temperature inversion in place. Notice the smoke from wood-burning stoves and fireplaces trapped just above the city. Photo by author.

Warm fronts present hunters with an entirely different range of challenges and tactical options. Remember, if you could see the air mass interactions when a cold front moves through from the side, you would see an upward angled wedge of cold air near the ground displacing warm and moist air upward and "out of the way" much like a snowplow. Conversely, a warm front displacing cool air drags itself across the landscape like a sharply angled broom across a garage floor. In a "normal" atmospheric state the temperature gets cooler the higher up you go, but the profile of a warm front is such that, for a period of time prior to the front's arrival, the air at altitude will be warmer than it is at the surface until the front moves through. This is one scenario that creates what is called a "temperature inversion" where cool air is trapped near the ground and a layer of warm air lies above it. This warm air layer acts like a lid on the air near the ground, trapping smoke, smog and other pollutants underneath it. In the late fall and winter months, this kind of atmospheric situation can result in air quality alerts for urban areas. For the hunter far from town, it presents strategic options.

Before we look in detail at hunting related to warm fronts, I need to cover a bit of information about clouds. There are four basic categories of clouds, and they are cirrus, stratus, cumulus and nimbus. Primarily two things distinguish cloud types: Their altitude and their appearance. High wispy clouds are composed of ice crystals instead of water droplets. These are cirrus clouds usually found at 20,000 feet or higher. Clouds that form a layer of overcast at any level of the atmosphere are called stratus, sometimes used as a prefix in the form of strato as in stratocumulus (an overcast layer of merged cumulus clouds) Clouds that show vertical development, appearing as giant cotton balls or cauliflowers are cumulus clouds. Any cloud producing precipitation has a variation of nimbus inserted into its name.

Don't get flustered. It's not really as complicated as it seems. A cumulus cloud that is producing rain becomes a cumulonimbus cloud and is often associated with thunderstorms. Stratus clouds that form in the mid levels of the atmosphere are altostratus clouds. Very high, thin overcast is usually made up of cirrostratus (combining cirrus with stratus) clouds. A low overcast is simply called stratus, but if it is raining it is called nimbostratus. Clouds associated with a cold front passage are usually in relatively close proximity to the front and tend to be cumulus in nature. There may be a period of overcast that is likely stratocumulus or nimbostratus. Clouds associated with an approaching warm front are far more varied and can be seen hundreds of miles ahead of the front. A hunter in a field with a warm front approaching is likely to first notice high cirrus clouds that will eventually form into a high overcast made up of cirrostratus clouds. As the

Stratocumulus clouds near Bridgeport, Nebraska. Photo by author.

"Altocumulus clouds over Box Butte Reservoir in northwest Nebraska. Photo by author.*

Cumulonimbus clouds over Badlands National Park in South Dakota. Photo by author.

Nimbostratus clouds over the Nebraska Panhandle. Photo by author.

High cirrus clouds can precede an approaching warm front by several hundred miles, but they can also form a shorter distance ahead of storm clouds associated with a cold front or thunderstorms. Photo by author.

cloud deck lowers from the high to the mid levels of the troposphere ahead of the advancing front, it will become composed of altostratus clouds. Once those clouds start to produce precipitation they become nimbostratus with the deck becoming increasingly lower until the front finally passes. Because warm fronts move considerably slower than cold fronts, the weather produced by them lingers longer until they finally pass through. Precipitation also tends to be more steady and consistent, lasting several hours instead of a few. Very heavy precipitation is generally not characteristic of a warm front, though it's not impossible, but long-term, steady precipitation is. If you rise before dawn to head out to your hunting ground and notice steady rain or drizzle falling, make a quick check of a few other weather parameters. In North America, winds prior to the passage of a warm front will have an easterly component, becoming south or southwest after the front moves through. Barometric pressure will be slowly and steadily falling ahead of a warm front, contrasted with the often-rapid drop in pressure prior to a cold front's arrival. Visibility may be reduced in fog, drizzle or mist ahead of a warm front, and when the appointed time for dawn arrives, expect a low lead-colored overcast.

Deer are active in weather ahead of a warm front so long as any precipitation that may precede the front is relatively light.

A communications device or GPS unit capable of receiving National Weather Service bulletins and forecasts can be a valuable asset to hunters in the field, especially when weather conditions seem to be changing and an updated forecast is needed. Photo by author.

The dew point temperature and relative humidity will climb steadily as the front approaches. It helps to have consulted the latest forecast the evening before the hunt to know if a warm front is on the way, but if you're miles from the nearest TV set, don't have a NOAA weather radio receiver or GMRS radio capable of receiving NOAA information, and the conditions I've just described exist at the deer camp, then it's time to mobilize in warm front hunting mode. Just what does that mean? For one thing, 100% waterproof yet breathable outerwear with some kind of human scent inhibitor is not optional.

Unlike the cold front scenario in which I'd have to give a clear advantage to the spot-and-stalk deer hunter over his quarry, the warm front is a double-edged sword that cuts both ways when it comes to who has the advantage. Scent lingers in moist, humid air and any fog, mist or drizzle will cause scents to linger even more on vegetation. For the hunter without any scent inhibitors, the path to the deer stand will be announcing his or her presence to any animal that crosses it for hours after it's been walked. But the moist air's scent-transmitting properties can also serve the well-prepared hunter. Hours preceding the passage of a warm front are excellent for the use of scent attractants for the same reasons I've just outlined. Add to those the tendency for warm fronts to trap particles in the atmosphere near the surface, and you have the best possible scenario for deploying a Buck Bomb, Tink's scents, doe-in-heat liquids, buck lure scents and just about anything else you can legally use. Winds ahead of a warm front tend to be much lighter than those ahead of and behind a cold front, so whatever scents you can deploy will be concentrated near the point of deployment and gently spread out in a westerly direction. Whereas I recommend a spot-and-stalk strategy following the passage of a cold front, I give the warm front advantage to the still hunters and stand hunters. Let's look at an effective strategy situation.

When a property owner gives permission to hunt, always ask if it's okay to set up more than one portable blind or stand. If it is permitted, and you have the resources, I recommend setting up four stands or blinds with one on each compass point north, south, east, and west of a known deer feeding area. There are a number of reasons for this recommendation, but a primary one is that wind seldom blows precisely from these directions in North America. Wind seems always to blow from a direction between two compass points such as southeast, northwest, southwest and northeast. If the landowner only gives permission for one blind or stand, put it on the east side of the feeding area, but remember that it's critical to wear a layer of clothing that contains or eliminates human scent from head to toe for the strategy I'm suggesting to work. The recommended position to the east places the sun at your back at dawn (prime time for hunting). You'll have a clear view of deer in a field west of you while they will have to look right into the sun to see you, and on days when a warm front is coming with wind direction anywhere from southeast to northeast, deployed scent lures will entice lovesick bucks in the field to your west to approach the tree line or cover you're using for concealment. Even if the wind is from southeast through northeast all day, the scent lures will be working hard for you the whole time. The only damper on this plan is precipitation. If rain or drizzle is steady, your attractant scent will be pushed lower and lower on vegetation and eventually onto the ground where it will be gradually diluted. Its scent also won't carry as far when it's raining or snowing. This can be overcome by occasional deployment of more scent attractants during the day, if feasible without betraying your position, but keep in mind that unless you're covered head-to-toe in clothing that stops your human scent from escaping, you'll be mixing it up with anything you deploy and a big, wary buck will know something isn't right.

If legal in your area, this deer-hunting scenario I've created is also an excellent opportunity to use a full-bodied deer decoy. Remember that visibility ahead of a warm front's approach is often reduced, both for you and the deer. The combination of an attractive doe-in-heat scent along with a glimpse of what appears to be a receptive doe

Unless precipitation becomes heavy, the weather associated with a warm front usually won't shut down normal deer social and feeding activity.

near the place the scent seems to be coming from may just be the added enticement needed to bring a dominant buck in close for a good shooting opportunity.

Unlike what happens with strong cold fronts, deer activity doesn't seem to shut down as dramatically when warm fronts approach, and it resumes as normal almost immediately once the warm front passes. While deer will move into cover if precipitation becomes heavier, the presence of light rain, snow and drizzle doesn't seem to deter them from regular feeding and social activity. Enhanced scent transmission and comparatively still conditions that precede a warm front still give them smell and hearing as defenses against danger, even though their visual acuity may be impaired. Deer are also on the move when such atmospheric conditions are present, making good opportunities for stand and still hunters so long as they remember to conceal their scent.

One thing that a moister environment does for spot-and-stalk hunters is to help deaden the sound of movement. Wet vegetation and wet leaves on the forest floor don't snap, crackle and pop like they do when it's dry. The water in the air is an excellent sound transmitter, and any Navy veteran will tell you how much more effectively sounds are transmitted underwater than above, but in order for sound to be transmitted there has to be a noise. Scent-eradicating layers teamed with a very quiet, tightly woven, water-resistant bushed-fleece shell, or a shell made of similar material, will enable the spot-and-stalk hunter to move quietly without being winded. Unfortunately, the "spot" part of spot-and-stalk can be hindered by reduced visibility, and the effectiveness of optics in precipitation can also be impaired. Over the years I've had mixed success employing a spot-and-stalk strategy in weather preceding a warm front, but better success still hunting in the vicinity of known feeding and high-deer-traffic areas.

There is a dark side to warm fronts, however, and that has to do with how much of a difference in temperature there is ahead of and behind the front in the late fall and early winter. If the warmer air is moving over a region that has been below freezing for some time, there is the chance that the warm front will produce rain at higher altitudes

Severe ice storms resulting from freezing rain can wreak havoc with transportation, communication and utilities. Ice from freezing rain can accumulate very quickly and the only course of action a hunter has is to be where he or she intends to spend a day or two when the freezing rain starts. If caught in the field when freezing rain begins unexpectedly, get to safe shelter as quickly as possible and don't attempt to weather the storm outside. Hypothermia would be a real danger for a hunter caught in a remote area during an ice storm.
Photo courtesy of NOAA's National Weather Service Online Collection. Public domain.

that will turn to sleet as it falls through the colder air nearer the ground. If the cold air layer near the surface is not very thick, the liquid rain will fall, cool and then freeze on contact with surfaces that are below freezing at ground level. This is the dreaded freezing rain or ice storm. If the precipitation is hard enough and long enough, the weight of ice accumulating on tree branches and power lines can cause them to snap. Do not attempt to hunt deer in an ice storm. You're taking your life in your hands driving to and from your hunting location, getting into or out of an ice-covered elevated stand is extremely dangerous, you may have trouble walking and risk injury as a result of a fall, your equipment may freeze up and fail to function, and the deer will be holding tight in cover.

Once the warm front has moved through an area, weather conditions tend to improve rapidly. Temperatures climb, it remains humid, but precipitation generally shuts down, snow and ice melt, and the overcast lifts or clears. Barometric pressure will rise a bit and then stabilize, and winds come around to blow from the south to southwest. The air mass behind the front is usually somewhat unstable, and the warm front is most likely associated with a low-pressure system somewhere to the west that also has a cold front associated with it. The length of time between the passage of the warm front and arrival of the cold front can be hours or more than a day, but when the cold front gets closer to your hunting ground, the winds will increase, pressure will start to drop and, depending on the season and atmospheric conditions ahead of the cold front, there will be the possibility of thunderstorms.

The interval of time between the passage of the warm front and arrival of the cold front can offer excellent

hunting. Deer will be out, active and feeding aggressively to get as much in their paunch as possible before the cold front arrives. The weather is mild and can be very comfortable for hunters, but winds will increase from a southerly and eventually southeasterly direction as the cold front gets closer and barometric pressure starts to fall again more rapidly.

There are two kinds of weather fronts that we have not yet looked at. One is the stationary front, and the other is the occluded front. As its name implies, the stationary front means that little or no change is expected on either side of it. For the hunter that means the deer will continue to behave as they have been until a weather system either develops along the stationary front to mobilizes it or the front ceases to exist. The occluded front is a far nastier weather element for both man and beast to have to deal with.

Because cold fronts move faster than warm fronts around low-pressure centers, eventually the cold front will overtake the warm front and the section of the storm system where this takes place is called an occlusion. Without getting into a whole lot of meteorological mumbo jumbo here, let's just say that the occluded front, the leading edge of the occlusion and what comes behind it combine the worst elements of both warm and cold fronts as they pertain to the comfort of hunters and other mammals. Potentially gusty winds, prolonged precipitation (potentially heavy at times), colder temperatures and overcast conditions dominate the weather. In late fall and winter these weather factors can combine to cause blizzard conditions or, in southern states, prolonged periods of wind-blown rain. An ethical hunter knows his or her limitations. Those limitations will be different for each of us, and each weather situation is different. I can't tell you not to hunt when an occluded front is bearing down on your hunting area because your hunting area may be a couple hundred acres relatively close to shelter while another hunter's favorite deer ground might be public land high in the mountains miles from the nearest shelter. What I can tell you is that occluded storm systems are usually rather strong, tend to be slow moving over the United States, and can produce the most extreme weather conditions you're likely to ever hunt deer in if you decide to hunt. Good gear, common sense and survival skills will get you through, but the only way you're going to bag a deer in such conditions is to stalk through areas you think they might be hiding in and jump them. That's when you'll make an interesting observation.

Normally deer will flee into the wind so that all of their defensive senses of sight, smell and hearing can be employed to direct them away from a threat. Wind-blown precipitation can alter this behavior. Photo copyright by The Black Hills Pioneer Newspaper. Used by permission.

Normally, when you jump a deer that is bedded in cover it will run away from you into the wind so its nose and eyes can sense the presence of danger in its path. Of course, if you're part of a line of slug-gun hunters driving deer through field of crops, the deer will cut away to the right or left as soon as they sense the presence of any blocker waiting in ambush. But as a general principle, a deer will flee from you into the wind immediately or turn into the wind as it flees.

The exception to this rule is hunting in wind-blown precipitation, the kind you're likely to encounter with an occluded front or a strong cold front. A deer does not like to run 30 mph headlong into sleet, rain or snow for any great distance. Imagine how your face would feel if you were running at that speed into ice pellets coming at you at the same speed from the opposite direction, in essence hitting your eyes, ears and nose at 60 mph. At that speed even raindrops can sting. Any precipitation striking these highly sensitive portions of a deer's defensive systems essentially shuts them down and the animal is running "blind." For that reason, a deer jumped in wind-driven precipitation will either flee with the wind immediately, or quickly turn in that direction. I won't argue about taking running shots here. Some hunters will, some won't. For those that do, this little tidbit of information will tip you off so you're ready and know which way a jumped deer is going to go. Also, a deer is not likely to run as far as it would in other kinds of weather. It will likely head for the nearest available cover at what it feels is a "safe distance" away from you, and there it will hold tight again. If you're very familiar with your hunting ground, you will know where these shelter areas are located, and could have a chance to jump the deer a second time should you miss the first opportunity.

To summarize what we've covered pertaining to deer hunting in relation to weather fronts, here are the main points to remember. Cold fronts can bring quick change, high winds after they pass, and periods of heavier precipitation that are for the most part short-lived. Deer will be active and feed aggressively prior to the arrival of a cold front, and then move to cover once the front moves through and remain relatively inactive until things settle down. The best hunting tactics are to spot-and-stalk upwind toward areas you think deer may be waiting out the winds.

Warm fronts bring more gradual change with increasing clouds and a lowering cloud deck. Winds tend not to be as strong as with cold fronts and front-induced temperature inversions make the use of scent lures effective unless there is steady precipitation. Visibility may be reduced in drizzle, light rain and snow, or fog, and if conditions are right there is the possibility of freezing rain or drizzle until the front passes. Still and stand hunting is a good choice as deer tend to follow their usual behavioral patterns and will be moving around unless the precipitation gets too heavy in open areas, in which case they will move to cover. The interval of time between the passage of a warm front and arrival of the next cold front can offer superb deer-hunting weather.

Stationary fronts have little impact on deer behavior. If you've observed certain patterns of behavior in a particular herd or deer in a certain area, the presence of a stationary front is unlikely to interrupt those patterns.

Occluded fronts bring the worst weather elements for both man and beast. Wind, extended periods of precipitation that may be heavy, falling temperatures, rising

A splendid buck in a Nebraska wheat field before the arrival of a cold front. Photo by Justin Long

barometric pressure and slow weather-system movement can mean a miserable day or two in the field, if it's even safe to hunt in the first place. Powerful late-fall occluded systems can bring blizzard conditions with reduced visibility in blowing snow. Precipitation may start as rain and then turn to sleet or snow. Those up to the challenge of hunting in such conditions need to be aware of the risks and well equipped to deal with changing and potentially extreme weather conditions. The best hunting tactics will be spot-and-stalk into the wind to try to flush deer from cover. Occluded fronts can be hard on both hunters and their gear, so be careful and always have a fall-back plan.

CHAPTER 4

Breaking Wind

Wind is air in motion. For most hunters, the concept of wind is simply that. They'll find out what direction the wind is blowing from and adjust strategy accordingly to prevent their scent from being sniffed by wary deer before they can close the distance for a shot. There is nothing wrong with this understanding of wind apart from the fact that it is incomplete. For the deer hunter the biggest influences that wind has on the hunt are its ability to carry scent and sound, and also to alter the course of projectiles. What

"Hunting is a family affair for the author. His son, Alex, served as deer spotter and shooting stick bearer on this successful hunt."

This mule deer buck was photographed spending the middle of his day just below the top of a ridge where visibility from high ground and upslope breezes could warn him of possible threats.

many hunters fail to consider, however, is that wind moves in three dimensions, not just two. Once hunters understand how wind interacts with surface terrain factors, they will be able to use the knowledge to enhance their chances of filling a freezer with venison.

Meteorologists use two important terms to describe air in motion. Advection is the horizontal movement of air. Convection is the vertical movement of air. What makes things very interesting is that advection and convection are constantly happening at the same time. This will involve breaking some long-held perceptions about wind and hunting. Consider the following example.

My wife and I had been applying for coveted Black Hills elk firearm season tags for years, but she was the lucky one who finally drew a tag. We scouted, talked with experienced elk hunters and then set out into western South Dakota's Black Hills National Forest where elk tags are few and issued only to state residents. Those fortunate enough to draw a tag must wait nearly a decade before getting a chance at another. In short, it's usually a "once-in-a-lifetime" experience.

The season was warm that year, and we hunted every chance we could get. The results were consistently the same. We started in the early mornings, hoping to catch a group of elk coming off the valley floors where they'd spent the night. They migrated uphill to spend the day relaxing on saddles just below the ridge tops between mountains. Inevitably, we'd find ourselves stalking very slowly uphill only to catch a fleeting glimpse of elk backsides racing away along the ridgeline, or we'd arrive at their beds minutes after their departure. Our stalks were silent, our approaches excellent, and wind was non-existent – or so we thought.

As the season drew to a close, it finally dawned on me what was happening to us. We were consistently being upsloped.

On the final evening of the season we turned the tables. Positioning ourselves near a small pond on a valley floor with fresh elk sign around it from the night before, we waited for the telltale signs of the evening downslope breeze to begin – a distinct sense of falling temperature and a "different" kind of smell to the air. We were patient. Then, with about 15 minutes of shooting light remaining, a young bull ran out of the woods and posed broadside almost precisely 100 yards from where we sat. My wife's Savage 110 rifle in .270 broke the evening stillness and in quick succession two holes were punched through the bull's ribcage scarcely two inches apart just behind his left shoulder. Hit though both lungs, the elk simply tipped over where he stood. We'd downsloped him.

Slope winds are something few hunters I know even think about until I mention it to them, but they're a part

of every wildland firefighter's basic training. Once these winds are explained to hunters, they suddenly realize, as my wife and I did, how and why certain stalks go wrong in mountainous or hilly terrain. Slope winds are more of a factor for hunters on otherwise "calm" days, and they have their greatest impact on hunting during the sunny, warmer, early-season bowhunts for deer and elk, and also during the autumn period known as "Indian summer."

On days you might call "calm" because you perceive little or no wind, the sun still heats the surface of the earth unevenly in hill country and by mid-morning the valley

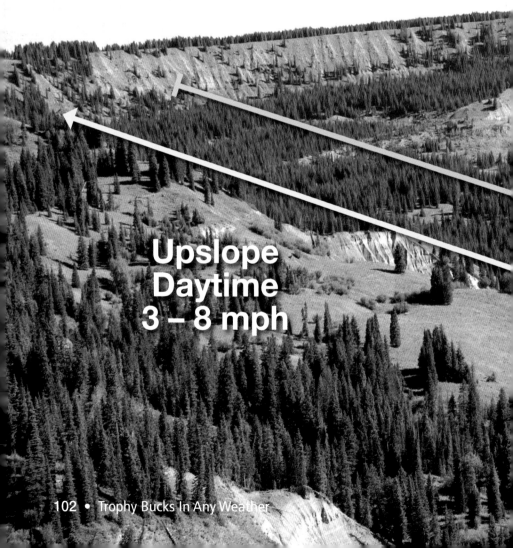

Upslope
Daytime
3 – 8 mph

floors tend to become warmer than the mountaintops and ridges. Given the natural tendency for warm air to rise, a subtle flow of air, at times hardly noticeable, begins to blow uphill at average speeds of only 3 to 8 miles-per-hour. In forested areas, beneath a canopy of trees, spot-and-stalk hunters may not even be aware that this gentle flow of air is carrying their human scent and sounds uphill. But deer and elk know, and that's one reason why they like to relax up on the high ground in saddles and plateaus during the day. The combination of upslope airflow carrying scent to their

Downslope
Evening – Overnight
2 – 5 mph

nostrils from all sides of the hill below them teamed with the sight advantage afforded by the high ground and the faint sound of a hunter huffing and puffing, no matter how quietly, in an attempt to climb up gives hunting uphill in the middle of the day a low-percentage success rate.

The slope winds start to reverse in the later afternoon when the sun sinks lower in the sky. The hillsides start to lose the heat acquired during the day, usually faster on the east-facing slopes. Any hunter who has spent days in the

mountains knows exactly what I'm talking about because he or she has felt that quick late-day switch that brings cooling to the air while standing on the side of a hill. With it usually comes a fresh scent, a subtle but different "feel" to the air from the way it's been all day. That switch is the hunter's clue that the downslope airflow cycle has begun.

Downslope flow is usually weaker than upslope flow at less than 5 mph, and the force that drives it is primarily gravity because the cooler the air, the denser it is and the

Hunters, wildlife watchers, firefighters and nature photographers will all be well served by understanding the 3-D nature of wind as manifested in upslope and downslope breezes in hilly or mountainous terrain. Photo by author.

faster it sinks. Because higher elevations cool more quickly than the valleys in the evening, the descending flow gives the advantage to the properly positioned hunter for all the same reasons upslope did to the game animals during the day. Often, a hunter who has done his or her homework can position himself or herself in the right place for an ambush as deer and elk head down to the valleys for water, food and the advantage of winding or hearing predators approaching from the mountains or steep hills around them. It's not uncommon for such hunters to hear or smell the approaching game even before it is seen. That's how my wife got her elk. At this point you may be asking if hunting during the day in the mountains is useless given the nature of upslope winds. Is it better to just find an ambush point on a trail and head out to it in the early afternoon? No. Just use the information I've given you to your advantage.

Keep in mind that the effect of upslope and downslope air movement can be negated by strong surface winds associated with approaching fronts and storm systems. The scenarios I've described above are most pronounced during warm and sunny days when high pressure is in firm control of the atmosphere over the hunt area and conditions are otherwise apparently calm. By paying close attention to predicted weather conditions in your hunting area, you can know 24 hours in advance if upslope or downslope winds might play a factor. If you think they will, then develop tactics accordingly.

Being in position near a known high-ground big-game bedding area before sunrise can defeat upslope. This might mean establishing a spike camp on the mountain some distance from the bedding area the night before, or heading up to the high ground very early in the morning before game moves up the mountain. Try these tactics during

preseason scouting to see if they work. If you get a later start in the morning, it may be more productive to spend the day searching the valley floors for areas of high game traffic and sign from the night before. Then get into position early in the afternoon so you're ready if game returns to the area once the downslope kicks in mid- to late-afternoon. Just remember that the air around you is almost always in motion in mountainous or hilly terrain, even if it is barely perceptible. Understanding when, where and how that air moves can help you defeat the natural defenses of smell, sight and hearing possessed by your quarry.

The upslope and downslope wind flows can, however, be limited by such things as temperature inversions and the fact that air cools at roughly 3°F to 5°F for every 1,000-ft. of increase in altitude (depending on a variety of atmospheric conditions). This means that there may be a thermal "ceiling" to the upslope flow and it may not extend all the way to the top or even the saddles in high mountain ranges such as the Rockies, Cascades, Big Horns and several Alaskan ranges.

Deer hunters in mountainous terrain with lower peaks such as the Black Hills, Ozarks, Appalachians, and areas with similar elevation differences, however, will find knowledge of upslope and downslope winds very useful.

Hunters must think about wind flow three dimensionally, and to do so I find it helpful to explain this concept by thinking of air movement in the same way we think of water movement. We hunt in the lowest level of the atmosphere, the bottom of the troposphere known by meteorologists as the boundary layer. In the boundary layer, air moving over surface objects can have its course affected by terrain features. We have to remember that, though invisible and seemingly lightweight to us, the air in which we move around is itself constantly in motion and has mass. Therefore, as air moves across an area, the lowest levels of that air encounter friction with the ground that impacts the way it flows. Above the boundary layer, the layer impacted by Earth's surface features, air can move freely and relatively uninfluenced by surface terrain. Now, if I'm starting to lose you here, let me use an illustration to make this more easily understood.

Think of the last time you were on the bank of a clear stream watching the water ripple over the rocky bottom. Visualize the scene in your mind. Some of those rocks on the bottom were larger than others, some reaching up high enough so that the current carried water both over and around them. Perhaps there were even boulders that were half underwater and half above the surface. Now think about the way the water moved over and around the rocks.

As water encounters a rock obstacle's upstream side, some water flows around the obstacle to the right, some to the left and some over the top. The displaced water

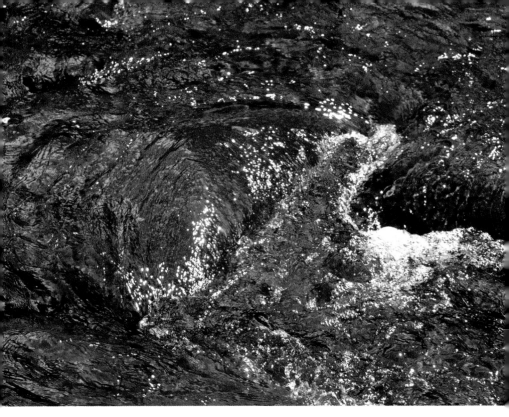

Movement of air around hills and mountains is not unlike the movement of water in a stream around boulders and rocks. Studying this movement as it relates to certain shapes and sizes of rocks in a stream can give insight as to how winds might move around or over terrain where you hunt. Photo by Author.

then converges on the downstream side of the rock and, depending on the size and shape of the rock, it will either create a small swirling eddy that continues downstream before it dissipates, or there will seem to be a permanently established area of turbulent backflow on the downstream side of the rock where the converging water seems to try to back up into the rock and even climb its downstream face.

Perhaps you've experienced something similar on a river-rafting trip as you go through a stretch of rapids. As the raft flows over or around decent-sized rocks in class III or higher rapids, sometimes the back of the raft gets pulled rearward toward the rocks and into the churning waters only to be shot rapidly out as the oarsman does his or her job. Having contemplated these two examples of the stream and the raft, now think about how wind interacts with terrain structure in the areas you hunt.

The extent to which wind interacts with surface objects and the degree to which such interaction affects deer hunters is directly related to the size of the object and the strength of the wind. For the Kansas whitetail hunter hiding in a shelterbelt adjacent to a field of crops in the middle of otherwise open, flat country the temptation might be to think this has nothing to do with you. But a

Mature shelterbelts and windbreaks made up of trees no only hold deer, but can also disrupt prevailing wind flow near the ground on a smaller, more localized scale. Trail camera photo courtesy of John Dunlap.

row of tightly planted trees acting as a shelterbelt is there for a reason, and that reason is to disrupt linear wind flow at ground level. Shelterbelts may not be a solid as mountains, buttes and hills, but if they are dense enough they will disrupt winds in a similar, albeit potentially diminished manner. For hunters using portable blinds in such a hunting situation, the place to set up shop would be on or just inside the tree line on the downwind side of the shelterbelt. By doing so, you place yourself in that area of turbulent backwash demonstrated in my two water examples. And on windy days you'll have less of a chance that manmade scents and noises will be blown from the shelterbelt onto the field where the deer are expected to feed. Any deer walking toward you along the tree line from the right or left that did manage to catch a whiff of you would be confused about exactly where you would be because of the churning winds on the downwind side of the shelterbelt. That turbulence disables their ability to lock onto you precisely with their nasal radar, but they will be on heightened alert, so silence and minimal movement are important. Hunters using treestands or elevated blinds along shelterbelts want to be sure not to position them too high. As wind accelerates over the tops of the trees and moves more slowly through the lower levels of the vegetation, the higher your position the more likely your scent will be carried over the shelterbelt and onto the field your hunting stand overlooks.

I realize that some hunters might be asking whether or not consideration of such things is worth the time it takes to read them. After all, hunters have had great success in the past without thinking about all this technical wind flow stuff, so why give it a second thought? You may even be tempted to ask, "Who taught this guy this stuff anyway?" I first learned about it from a couple of mule deer bucks with 30+" inside antler spreads on a ranch strewn with buttes and shelterbelts in northwest South Dakota. They spent most of their days bedded down with their does on the leeward (that's downwind) side of small hills and buttes about 5-10 yards downhill from the crest. To put it more simply, I learned this stuff from some pretty big and wise old bucks, along with some input from meteorology professors.

Western mule deer are pretty clever as deer go, and the rancher in charge of the place where I'd been watching these bucks explained their strategy. Given the vast open spaces, these mulies and their does selected these positions so that any danger approaching them downwind of their position would easily be seen coming from more than a mile away. Bedding down below the edge of the hilltop prevented them from being seen by all but the keenest-eyed predators or hunters outfitted with very good optics, as they were never silhouetted against the sky. Finally, any hunter trying to put the sneak on them upwind of their position would be either heard or scented as the wind flow carried noises and scents over the crest of the rise and into the noses of the deer on the opposite side. Though I was hunting antelope at the time, I did try to put the sneak on those mule deer bucks now and then just to see how close I could get by coming up over the top of the hill opposite the side on which they were bedded. I got busted every time. Then I figured something out.

I was working as a meteorologist for a TV station in Rapid City, South Dakota, at the time and was also helping a local Internet Service Provider produce a

Internet site about weather in the Black Hills region. In
the course of my research I visited the Department of
Atmospheric Sciences at the South Dakota School of
Mines and Technology. A professor there showed me some
ongoing work with computer models explaining how the
entire Black Hills geologic formation altered surface wind
patterns in the region and the relation of that alteration to
thunderstorm development initiation in a zone of leeside
wind convergence. Now before you go back and try to read
this paragraph over a few times to figure out what the heck
I'm trying to say, I'll put it another way.

   I figured what works on a big scale sometimes works

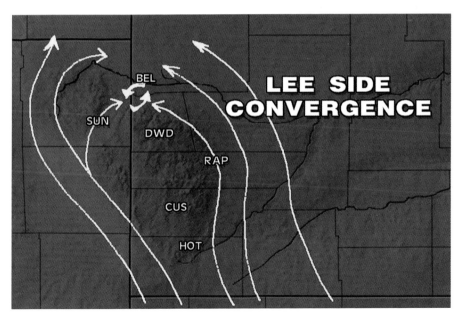

*The author used this computer graphic to demonstrate the principle
of wind flow around a mountain formation, in this case the
Black Hills of South Dakota, during a meteorology conference at
Mississippi State University. The three-letter identifiers represent
towns in the region. Much as a boulder would force water around
or over it, so too low-level winds are forced around and over
significant surface obstacles.*

on a small scale too, and what those scientists were doing with the computers was to discover what mule deer have probably known for centuries. Just like we figured from our stream examples, winds flowing around and over an object come together on the downwind side of that object, so if a deer sits on the downwind side of that object in the right place, he can pretty well hear or smell anything trying to creep up on him over the top or around the sides of the object.

Now at this point you may recall watching hunting videos or TV shows where a guide and his hunter client slide up over the lip of a canyon and catch a big-racked buck bedded just over the other side. If what I've been saying is true, how could they get that buck? It's all in the wind direction, stalk approach, and intelligence of the buck in question. Here's how to hunt a deer sitting below the lip of a canyon or steep hill with the wind at his back.

First of all, forget the idea of a frontal assault. Your camouflage may be good, but that big buck is up there with a mighty commanding view. You may be hunting into the wind so he can't smell you, but he'll sure see you and then the jig is up, especially if he's got does with him. You can also rule out stalking around behind him and approaching over the top of his perch if the prevailing surface wind will be at your back as you do so, and that is a crucial element. For the buck's security system to be effective, he has to be in a position where something approaching from over the canyon rim or hilltop will have wind blowing across it and into his nose and ears. If the wind is flowing along the side of the hill where the buck is bedded or blowing uphill toward him, then an over-the-top stalk will work, but extreme stealth is required covering those last few yards. If you come over the top to the right or left of the buck's position, he may see you before you see him and take off leaving you uttering colorful metaphors about running shots from a prone position.

I finally did close the distance on those mulies, even though I didn't have a mule deer tag, had no intention of shooting them and was unarmed at the time. I just wanted to try a plan to see if it worked. Instead of coming around the hill or over it with the wind at my back, I stalked within what would have been easy bow range by moving slowly uphill perpendicular to the wind direction while using the northeast-facing edge of the hill to hide me from view. Let me sketch it out more clearly for you. The deer were bedded on the northeast side of a hill with a light breeze blowing steadily from the southwest. I slipped into a saddle between the hill the deer were on and the one next to it southeast of their position, and then I slowly crept northwest. By staying slightly below the position of the deer, any wind carrying my scent would have wrapped around the deer's hill and the one behind me below the elevation where they were. It was late afternoon, so there was also a weak downslope flow to carry any indications of my pounding heart and sweating brow downhill away from the animals into the valley below. When the time came to make my move, I popped around the hillside less than 10 yards from the group of mulies and 10-20 feet downhill of their position. What's more, they were so stunned to see something as big as me so close to them that they froze for several seconds before reacting. If I had been on a mule

deer hunt, there would have been venison in the freezer and a superb mount on my wall. Instead, I got back to my antelope hunting.

Deer don't like it much when wind blows at moderate to high speeds, especially when they are in crops, trees or brush. I used to hunt deer in corn quite a bit on private land north of the Black Hills. The best days to hunt were when high pressure was still moving in behind a cold front that crossed the area a day or two before and winds of 10-20 mph or higher were still blowing.

It was just that kind of a day that my wife and I were hunting whitetails by peeking down rows of dry corn left standing in search of deer. Each of us had two tags to fill, one of which had to be an antlerless deer. The rows were about 600-yards long, and I spotted a large doe bedded halfway down one of the rows. The wind was from the northwest in the 10-20 mph range, and that was making the leaves on the stalks rustle quite a bit. In fact, it was downright noisy. We worked out a plan where I had my wife take up an ambush position west and a few rows over from the row the doe was bedded in. Then I worked around the stand of corn until I was northeast of the doe, slightly behind her and started moving slowly across the rows in the direction of the deer. By timing my movements to coincide with the higher gusts of wind, any noises I made as I brushed through the crops matched the rise in volume of the rustling corn leaves. Then, I started moving westward to let the doe catch a hint of my scent, know I was close, but be unable to use sight and sound to precisely pinpoint me due to the density of the corn and it's noise. The plan worked. The doe apparently discovered I was somewhere north of her and too close for comfort.

She rose and trotted out of the end of the corn rows barely 10 yards from where my wife was waiting with her trusty .270 Savage 110. The bullet found the doe's heart and she yielded a healthy quantity of fine-eating, corn-fed venison.

Windy days favor the spot-and-stalk hunter because they often produce conditions that make it easier to approach deer before being detected. If the wind isn't strong enough to force deer into cover, a threshold I put somewhere between 20 and 25 mph, they'll usually continue their routines so stand hunters along established trails can still do well in a bit of wind too. But the same noise factor that can aid a spot-and-stalk hunter means stand and still hunters will have to really be visually alert. The noise of wind blowing through the branches and rustling autumn leaves could mask the sound of a buck approaching on the deer trail.

Yet another kind of wind may be of concern for hunters pursuing deer in cover near the shore of a large body of water. If you've ever vacationed or hunted in the vicinity of any of the Great Lakes, large lakes such as Oahe in South Dakota, Fort Peck in Montana, Mille Lacs or Red Lake in Minnesota, and any one of a number of big bodies of water from Florida and Tennessee to Tahoe and Texas, you've probably noticed that the breeze always seems to be blowing off the water and into shore during the day while your campfire smoke column at night leans out toward the water. On inland waters this kind of wind is called a lake breeze, and in coastal areas it's a sea breeze. The distance inland from the shoreline where this kind of wind is of concern to hunters varies depending on the size of the body of water and the temperature of the water. Near large lakes such winds can affect areas up to 20 miles inland.

A decent lake breeze helped Phil Martin tag this nice Canadian caribou. Here's his story, "The caribou was taken on my first and only beach setup at about 1:00 p.m. while hunting in Nunavet, north of Manitoba. We spotted three bulls from the boat standing on an island point. They wanted to swim across to another island. We got the boat on shore, but could not get a shot by that time. Noticing all the fresh tracks on the beach, and their primary travel direction, we set up. The three bulls came back within 20 minutes to cross from the same point." By correctly setting up an ambush position inland from the caribou's path, the lake breeze blew Phil's scent inland and away from the animals as they walked along the beach.

I won't get too technical about what causes the wind to blow off the water during the day and toward the water at night. In simple terms, it has to do with the rate at which water and land absorb and lose heat. During the day, the sun warms the air over land faster because land soaks up the sun's heat at a faster rate. Warm air is less dense than cold air, so lower atmospheric pressure is created over the land than exists over the water and air always flows from high pressure toward low pressure. So air moves off the water and onto the land during the day. At night, the land loses heat faster than the water and the process is reversed. The cooler, denser air over the land flows out onto the lake. Since deer hunting at night is prohibited in most places, we'll focus on how lake breezes during the day can work for and against the deer hunter.

The lake breeze is of concern only to the extent that it is the dominant influence on air circulation in the area hunted. If a strong front or storm system is moving through a region, the winds produced by that weather system could override any lake breeze influences. For that reason, the lake breeze is of concern to hunters only on what might otherwise be a rather calm and sunny day during those portions of the season that they are hunting near open water.

It's not uncommon for stand and blind hunters to set up along deer trails that lead to water. The lake breeze will be strongest during the time of day that the temperature differences between the land and water are the greatest, and that's usually in the early afternoon. Therefore, lake breezes may not be of much concern for early morning and late afternoon hunters, but all-day hunters should take them into consideration. This is especially true when deer are active during the day because the rut is on. Hunters that set up along trails within sight of a large body of water need to understand that a lake breeze could tip deer off to their position by blowing human-caused scents inland along the trail during the day. Measures to counter this would include the use of scent-controlling layers of clothing, taking precautions to avoid scents such as human waste and foods being carried inland by the breeze during the midday, and the use of masking scents or scent lures and attractants as their odors would also be carried inland.

Most of what we've looked at so far about wind has to do with scent and sound detection. But there is yet another topic hunters must take into account when it comes to wind, and that is the role it plays on deflecting your projectile on its way to the deer. This influence on bullet and arrow flight is commonly known as wind drift, and it can be a very important consideration that means the difference between a quick, humane kill and wounding a deer or missing altogether.

The moment a bullet leaves the barrel or an arrow clears the rest there are a number of physical forces acting

on it. The force of gravity pulls it downward. The resistance of the air to its forward progress (known as drag) slows it down. The force of wind pushes a projectile off course. In my experience, many hunters underestimate just how profound an effect even relatively little wind can have.

In very general terms, the impact of wind on projectile flight depends on the size, shape and weight of the projectile, the duration of the flight and distance covered, and both the force and angle of the wind acting upon it. For bowhunters, arrow weight and length, the size of vanes and fletching, arrow speed, shot angle and so much more come into play. Given the highly customized nature of archery

Wind begins to influence the flight path of a bullet or arrow from the moment the projectile is shot. Photo by author.

equipment, I can only tell you from my personal experience with the modern, fast-shooting bow I use. Winds less than 20 mph don't seem to make a difference in hitting the kill zone on a deer inside of 20 yards. But 20-25 yards is my personal ethical range limit once crosswinds get up to around 20 mph, and that's with slim-profile carbon arrows. It is up to each archer to practice under a variety of wind conditions to arrive at his or her own maximum ethical range for taking game, and the only real way to know what that range is comes from lots of practice.

Rifle hunters can go on the Internet and purchase any one of several software programs available that will compute ballistics and print tables of information that include such things as velocity, bullet drop and wind drift. Some ammunition manufacturers offer such tables free of charge on their Web sites, one of which is Federal Premium Ammunition. To demonstrate the influence of a 10 mph crosswind, that is a 10-mph wind blowing directly across a bullet's flight either right to left or left to right, I used the Web site to produce wind-drift information for three popular deer calibers in the Federal Premium Vital-Shok line loaded with Nosler Ballistic Tip (NBT) bullets. Here is what the information revealed.

A .243 Winchester caliber 95-grain NBT bullet in the Vital-Shock line fired into a 10-mph crosswind will drift 3.2" at 200 yards, 7.6" at 300 yards and 14.2" at 400 yards. I won't argue for or against taking shots at 300 yards and beyond at this point, but will use those ranges for illustrative purposes. A 130-grain NBT in the .270-caliber Vital-Shok load fired under identical circumstances will be pushed 2.8" off course at 200 yards, 6.4" at 300 and 11.9" at 400 yards by a 10-mph crosswind. Finally, a 165-grain NBT

The only way for a shooter to know exactly what the wind is doing at the range or on a hunt is to take frequent personal observations with a weather instrument that's equipped with an accurate wind sensor (anemometer).
Photo by author.

fired from a .30-06 rifle using the Vital-Shok load will drift 2.8" at 200 yards, 6.6" at 300 yards and just over a foot at 400 yards. Now let's pick one range for these calibers and see what it tells us.

For all three calibers calculated using the specified ammunition and loads, the amount of wind drift at 300 yards was roughly between 6.5 and 7.5 inches, and that is for only 10 mph of crosswind. What if the wind was 13 mph? What if the angle of the wind in relation to the bullet path isn't 90 degrees, but 80 degrees? For years the standard for ethical hunting range has been the distance at which a hunter can consistently hit an 8" paper plate, and gives you 4" of leeway in any direction if you place your scope crosshairs dead center on the plate. As you can see from the information I've presented, even if any of these calibers were sighted in for a 200-yard zero and you compensated for bullet drop at 300 yards, a 10-mph crosswind would put you off the target plate to the right or left. If you took a 400-yard shot and correctly compensated for bullet drop but forgot about wind, a 10 mph crosswind would place your bullet 8-10 inches off the plate to the right or left. This is information every ethical hunter needs to know before taking exceptionally long shots. I'm not saying it cannot be done, and I know many accomplished shooters who can precisely tell you where their bullet will go at the ranges I've been using in this example and beyond in a wide range of wind conditions. Long-range competition shooters routinely hit their targets at extreme ranges, but only hours of practice with hundreds of rounds makes such shots consistently doable and ethical. And there is something else to keep in mind.

We have to remember that wind seldom blows steadily at any velocity. The weather observation for a given hour may say winds from a certain direction at "X" mph, but that only reflects conditions at the observation site at that point in time. In reality, winds at that site may be blowing at X plus or minus three or four mph. The only way a hunter can know precisely what the wind speed is at a certain location is to measure it with an accurate weather instrument. I carry a handheld unit leftover from my days as an assistant to the South Dakota state fire meteorologist and a member of the South Dakota Wildland Fire Suppression Division. It's a Kestrel 4000 that gives me a wide range of meteorological readouts including temperature, humidity, pressure, wind speed and more. Being extremely light and compact, it has a permanent place in my hunting pack right along with my GPS, knife, first-aid kit and other critical items. There are other manufacturers of handheld weather-sensing devices and which one you decide on is up to you, but I will tell

you that I don't head out on a hunt without mine. Every now and then I'll grab up a handful of grass or leaves and drop them about waist high to see which way the wind is blowing and if there's been a change since I last checked. Then I'll take out the weather device, face the wind wheel into the breeze and measure how fast it's blowing. For deer these days I shoot a 165-grain load in .30-06 and having on-site wind information at my disposal is very handy if I'm faced with a shot at a trophy buck standing 300 yards away.

So let's review how wind can play a role in the outcome of a deer hunt. First, we have to remember that there is a vertical component to wind, especially when hunting in hilly or mountainous terrain. Use the information presented on upslope and downslope winds to keep yourself from being busted and to bag that buck. Next, remember that terrain, shelterbelts and other objects on the ground can bend and turn wind. Use the noise wind generates to close the distance between you and the deer your hunting more effectively. Know how hunting the woods in the vicinity of large bodies of water can influence where your scent and the scent of your lures is carried during certain times of the day. Finally, remember that even a relatively small amount of crosswind can mess up your shot at longer ranges and learn how much you need to compensate for winds blowing at various speeds in order to hit your mark.

CHAPTER 5

Taking the Temperature

I can't think of any big-game animal in North America that is hunted in a wider range of temperatures than deer. You'll find deer in every state of our nation, making them one of the most adaptable creatures on the continent. They survive biting sub-zero cold in the forests of the Great Lakes region and on windswept plains between the Mississippi River and the Rockies. They endure blistering heat from the Desert Southwest across Texas. They contend with excessive rainfall in the Pacific Northwest and sweltering humidity across the South into the Everglades. During the deer seasons that typically take place in the fall and winter months, hunters venture into the fields and forests in weather that can include anything from snow and sleet to hail and heavy rain, and temperatures that range from those capable of afflicting unprepared hunters with frostbite in minutes to those that could bring heat exhaustion to hunters who fail to hydrate.

Chad Boyd and his dad, Tim, teamed up to bag this monster mulie during the 2005 Arizona muzzleloader season. Courtesy of Chad Boyd

Researching the subject of temperatures and deer behavior is a daunting task because they are far more capable of flourishing in extremes than humans are. I spent the first 30 years of my life in Minnesota living at an elevation of approximately 800 feet above sea level where summers were hot and humid and winters were snowy and bitter cold. My first deer hunts were in the cornfields of western Minnesota. It was there, on a windy and overcast day with temperatures in the 30s, that I harvested my first whitetail buck with a 12-gauge shotgun slug. From Minnesota I moved to the Black Hills region where I lived at an elevation some 3,000-ft. higher and the air was much drier. In time my body became acclimated to that region and summertime trips back to Minnesota seemed oppressively hot and muggy in the heavier air. My point is that our bodies get used to a certain environment, a certain range of temperatures and humidity that we associate with comfort. I suspect the same is true of deer, though they don't have the travel opportunities that humans do. I've often wondered how a whitetail buck from Texas would fare during his first winter in the Minnesota wilderness, were he to be transplanted there. How would a South Georgia whitetail handle eastern Montana? Could a Canadian mule deer survive his first summer in the Arizona desert? I'd guess that the deer would do fine as they've proved to be among the most adaptable animals on the continent. These are all hypothetical exercises but I present them to make a point.

Human beings in our natural state, without the help of air conditioning, heating or even clothing, can survive in only a very narrow range of temperatures. As a species I suspect we are far less robust than we once were. Then when you consider the deer, with little more than the fur on its back, and the extremes of the temperature in which it must live, you come to realize just how amazing and strong the animal is. But just because a deer has to endure in order to survive doesn't mean there are not conditions in which it is more comfortable than others.

These whitetails living on the northern edge of South Dakota's Black Hills endure summer heat near 100 degrees and subzero cold in the winter, yet they flourish. Such animals are a testimony to the heartiness of their species. Photo copyrighted by the Black Hills Pioneer Newspaper. Used by permission.

In preparing this book, I digested information from countless studies and articles written by individuals varying in their level of expertise from amateur to PhD. I concluded that while there is no shortage of information that has been gathered about the deer of North America, we probably still have as much or more to learn about them as we've discovered thus far. One of the secrets to how deer flourish seems to be that they are constantly in the process of adapting. Everything from coat thickness to food requirements and activity levels not only varies from one geographic region to another, but also from season to season and even from animal to animal within a specific herd based on gender and individual animal health. For that reason, I have to approach the subject of deer behavior in relation to temperature with caution.

As I stated at the beginning of this book, its contents are largely based on my personal observations of deer within a relatively small geographic area. I am confident that the behavioral patterns and strategies I've suggested thus far are solid and applicable for most deer hunters, but when it comes to temperatures I have to leave room for other writers and researchers to draw additional conclusions that may differ from my own. Let me give you a specific example of what I mean.

The deer in my area of study from the northern Black Hills onto the adjacent plains were most active when the temperature was between 28 degrees and 59 degrees. That doesn't mean there was no activity at all when it was colder or warmer, only that the deer I observed seemed to "prefer" that temperature range for being active and doing what deer do. I fully expect that someone researching a deer herd in south Texas may arrive at a different temperature range because it seldom gets down to 28 degrees and gets a whole lot hotter than 59 in that part of the country. Similarly, a researcher in Michigan's Upper Peninsula or central Saskatchewan may arrive at a lower temperature range for peak deer activity because it's often colder in those places. If you forced me to narrow the range further, I'd tell you that deer around the Black Hills seem to love it when it's between 45 and 60 degrees, and that goes for both mulies and whitetails.

One thing that I share in common with the deer I observed is that we hate to be hot. I've tried hunting a few times when Indian Summer was on full force and the temperature was near 80 degrees in the early afternoon, but I never got anything but sweaty and thirsty. Deer activity levels dropped way off when it got hot outside.

This Black Hills area buck is quite relaxed and in no particular hurry. It's the kind of behavior frequently observed by the author when watching deer in hot weather. Photo copyrighted by the Black Hills Pioneer Newspaper. Used by permission.

They waited longer before coming out to feed in the late afternoon, fed longer into the evening, and didn't stay out as long feeding in the morning once the blazing sun rose above the trees. While I have no scientific evidence to base my next statement on other than my personal observation, they also seem "lazier" in hot weather, as if they were in some kind of energy conservation mode. The deer seemed to move slower (unless spooked, in which case they would flee as normal), and their reaction times didn't seem as

A thunderstorm moved through the Black Hills one warm afternoon during bow season, displaying a pair of rainbows as it left the area. Deer were already relaxing in the cover of the dry creek bed in the lower right portion of the picture, taking advantage of the tall grass and shade offered by a few trees when the storm moved through. Such natural drainages with shade and scattered pools of water offer hunters excellent places to wait in ambush nearby. Eventually deer will come out to feed in the adjacent fields. Photo by author.

sharp as what I was used to seeing on colder days.

What really puzzled me on those hot days was that for the longest time I couldn't figure out where the deer went when the heat was on. My usual spot-and-stalk tactics failed to spot or jump so much as a yearling. Eventually I came to learn that some of them were bedding in the tall grass on islands in the river along the property boundary. The water depth varied from about six inches to three feet through most of that stretch of water. Then when the heat subsided in the late afternoon and the sun dipped close to the horizon, I'd see the deer almost magically appear in the adjacent fields as if beamed into them by some Star Trek transporter device. Based on my observations, a hot-weather hunt with temperatures above 80 degrees is a low-percentage hunt for the hunter confined to open fields and prairies. If the weather forecast predicts hot weather, my advice is to limit your hunting to the early morning and late afternoon to avoid frustration and overheating yourself, or try very slow spot-and-stalk tactics through heavily shaded shelterbelts, creek bottoms and cover near water.

Sometimes we can't pick and choose the days we hunt and only have a few on which we can fill our tags. If you're unfortunate enough to have your hunt fall in the middle of a heat wave, look for possible ambush positions near water and wait. A typical whitetail deer needs about 4-5 quarts of water a day, but remember that it doesn't need to get all of that from lakes, ponds, stock tanks and streams. Dew, condensed moisture and food sources with a high water content also count toward a deer's daily water intake needs. During your preseason scouting, look for areas that still have lush, green vegetation as a possible source of both food and water for deer, and be sure to check those areas if the weather really heats up. You might get lucky and spot a buck chewing cud in a shady green spot.

Another reason I don't like to hunt in hot weather has to do with the urgency involved in getting game dressed, skinned and cooled down as much as possible. There are differing opinions as to how long a hunter has before meat spoilage begins to ruin venison during warm-weather hunts, and this is of particular concern to bowhunters because of the warm weather often encountered during the early season. Fortunately, most deer harvested during

Because deer were taking a heavy toll on his haystacks, a northwest South Dakota rancher was more than willing to let the author's hunting party use his tractor's bale loader as an impromptu outdoor meat locker after a successful morning hunt. Getting your deer up off the ground and opened up to cool is an excellent way to retard the onset of meat spoilage. Photo by author.

those early days of the season are taken in the morning when it's still relatively cool, or in the evening when it's only going to get colder. Rather than debate the time factor involved, the important things to remember are to field dress your deer as quickly as possible, open up the body cavity so that air can circulate inside, use paper towels to clean out any blood or fluids and keep the animal clean, dry and in a shady spot until you can get it skinned completely and hung in a cool place. Use of cheesecloth

The author poses with a western diamondback rattlesnake (deceased) during a wild hog hunt in southwest Texas. Snakes are a threat in some parts of the country year-round. Notice the author's snakeproof gaiters and steel-toed boots for added insurance. Photo by Rob Graham.

or fine mesh meat socks can also help keep flies and other insects off your meat without hindering air circulation. Keep in mind that warm temperatures, along with moisture and dirt, are a leading cause of game meat spoilage and contamination.

One last observation about warm-weather hunting has to do with hazards hunters face from other creatures. Bow seasons, early upland game seasons and some youth deer seasons take place when it is still mild enough for snakes and biting insects to be out. Hunters can be at risk to contract insect-transmitted illnesses such as West Nile virus and lyme disease, and should take precautions. New bugproof clothing technology offers one kind of protection against mosquitoes and biting flies, and there are a number of effective repellents on the market. The best defense against snakes is to remind yourself of their presence if you hunt in snake habitat, and then tread carefully as you stalk. Most of the time a snake is just as eager to avoid you as you are to avoid it and will escape if given the option. If a guide or outfitter warns you about the presence of venomous snakes in the area you'll be hunting, a decent pair of snake boots, snakeproof gaiters or snakeproof chaps is an excellent way to give yourself added protection. Being cold-blooded, snakes become lethargic in cool weather but can still cause a world of hurt if stepped on. Always be alert, but be especially so when hunting in temperatures warmer than 75 degrees and when walking back to the vehicle after sunset.

As late summer transitions into fall, deer activity in general increases. It isn't just that a rutting season is approaching, but rather that there is so much happening in the deer's environment as the days shorten and get cooler. The photosynthetic processes that keep the plants deer eat green and healthy are retarded as the hours of available sunlight become fewer. When the frosts arrive, green forage becomes brown and deer are constantly in search of new food sources. Often this search drives them to farms and ranches where crops and hay bales can make up for declining natural browse. With the shorter days, the temperatures cool and eventually the rutting season begins.

Does cold weather trigger the rut? I know a good many deer hunters who swear it does, while others believe the fall mating season is initiated by moon phase. What do I think? Based on my observations I do not believe that the arrival of cold weather alone initiates the rutting season. The arrival of cold weather is directly related to the shortening of daylight hours and the rutting season on the plains north of the Black Hills seems to begin pretty consistently around the second week of November whether the weather has been cold or not. Then again, we all have differing opinions as to what "cold" is depending on where we live. When I talk about cold weather in relation to deer hunting, I'm talking about days where the high temperature doesn't reach 40 degrees and overnight lows

The author remains unconvinced that cold weather, in and of itself, triggers the onset of the rutting season. Trophy bucks are taken in both mild and cold conditions. A nice, sunny day didn't stop Kurt Kaiser from bringing down this thick-necked Nebraska whitetail with his bow in 2006. Photo courtesy of Kurt Kaiser. Used by permission.

are in the teens or colder. But I have seen intense rutting action in November when high temperatures were in the 50s for several days. To say that the mating season won't "really get going" until cold weather arrives and stays for awhile is, I think, oversimplifying a complex process that is more instinctive and primal than we realize. I believe a combination of factors is likely involved that brings does into estrus, and though temperature may be one of those

factors, we have yet to fully understand what all the other factors involved are. My support for this statement comes from observing a few rutting seasons that came and went without the arrival of cold weather until they were pretty much over. Other years I've seen bitter cold temperatures pour through the area around Halloween only to be followed by a warm up, and the rut didn't seem to begin any earlier. I have, however, noticed that the rut does

When fall arrives and natural browse becomes more scarce, deer move into suburban areas or encroach on farms and ranches in greater numbers to take advantage of manmade food sources. Photo copyrighted by the Black Hills Pioneer Newspaper. Used by permission.

seem to last a bit longer when it coincides with a stretch of relatively mild temperatures, about 10 degrees above the normal for the time of year, and that the rut is shorter but more intense when colder than average temperatures dominate the region for an extended period. Whether this observation is universal across the nation I can't say, but it certainly seems to be the case on the western High Plains.

The areas where I have spent most of my time deer hunting over the last couple of decades have largely been privately owned farms and ranches with streams or rivers running through or near the property. Such an environment couldn't be better for deer. The lands contained both abundant natural forage from the grasses, oaks and other vegetation along the river bottoms. When natural food was in short supply, there were always dozens of big, round hay bales on almost every property. There were a few seasons when the corn crop was either still standing or had just been harvested when the first bitter blasts of Arctic air

moved in, and there's nothing deer like better than corn on the cob. Like humans, deer have a taste for "fast food" and don't want to work any harder for a meal than they have to. For that reason, my hunts during bitter cold weather focused on bedding places nearest a manmade food source.

The reasoning behind this strategy is fairly simple. Deer need to maintain a certain metabolic rate along with sufficient energy reserves to make it through the winter. Digging through snow for food and trudging through deep snow sap a deer's energy, and so does exposure to the cold. Therefore, when a deer beds down after a morning feeding session, it is likely to do so in the most protected area it can find that will allow it to travel a relatively short distance back to the food source. On the land I hunted most, the three honey holes for bagging a bedded deer were a frozen cattail marsh, a river bottom and a dry irrigation ditch. All were within a few hundred yards of either crops or hay bales. On hunts when there was snow on the ground and temperatures were in the 20s, I could always count on finding a deer in one of those locations. They were below the general terrain or in standing crops, and therefore out of the chilly winds, and the brown vegetation those areas held provided great camouflage. Speaking of chilly winds, I need to address a few misconceptions about wind chill factors. I've read some articles that reference wind chill factors in relation to deer, but technically wind chill factors as we know them don't affect deer. Let me tell you why.

In the simplest terms, cold is the absence of heat. That which accelerates the loss of heat makes things that have heat lose it faster to environment. The wind chill factor was developed by the U.S. military during World War II to ascertain stresses and limitations various combinations of cold temperatures and wind placed on military personnel, and the onset of frostbite. After the Korean War the term "wind chill factor" began creeping into radio weather reports and eventually became a standard tidbit of information in TV and radio weathercasts from the 60s and 70s right on through today. What some hunter's fail to realize is that the wind chill factor has no effect on a hunter who is wearing a good layering system or quality insulated hunting clothes, boots, gloves and headgear. The wind chill factor, to be very blunt, only measures the heat robbing effect of the wind on a naked person. While I've heard of some guys getting primal and heading out to kill a boar with nothing but a spear and loincloth, I have yet to encounter a completely nude deer hunter in the field and pray that I never do.

Let's say the temperature outside is 38 degrees, but the wind chill factor is 20 degrees. That means that the wind flowing over an exposed human body at that given wind speed and temperature combination is removing heat from the naked human at the same rate as if the subject were standing in the same place on a perfectly calm day when the temperature was 20 degrees. Your gun, your truck's engine, and all the inanimate objects around you cannot get colder than the ambient temperature of 38 degrees. The water bottle on the side of your pack wouldn't even freeze, even with a wind chill factor well below freezing. All the wind will do is remove heat more quickly from inanimate objects and cool them down until their temperatures approach the ambient air temperature, but other variables involving the differences between humans and such objects prevent using the wind chill factor temperature to determine how quickly that heat

Wind Chill Chart

Photo courtesy of The National Weather Service.

Wind (mph)	Temperature (°F)																	
	40	35	30	25	20	15	10	5	0	-5	-10	-15	-20	-25	-30	-35	-40	-45
Calm	40	35	30	25	20	15	10	5	0	-5	-10	-15	-20	-25	-30	-35	-40	-45
5	36	31	25	19	13	7	1	-5	-11	-16	-22	-28	-34	-40	-46	-52	-57	-63
10	34	27	21	15	9	3	-4	-10	-16	-22	-28	-35	-41	-47	-53	-59	-66	-72
15	32	25	19	13	6	0	-7	-13	-19	-26	-32	-39	-45	-51	-58	-64	-71	-77
20	30	24	17	11	4	-2	-9	-15	-22	-29	-35	-42	-48	-55	-61	-68	-74	-81
25	29	23	16	9	3	-4	-11	-17	-24	-31	-37	-44	-51	-58	-64	-71	-78	-84
30	28	22	15	8	1	-5	-12	-19	-26	-33	-39	-46	-53	-60	-67	-73	-80	-87
35	28	21	14	7	0	-7	-14	-21	-27	-34	-41	-48	-55	-62	-69	-76	-82	-89
40	27	20	13	6	-1	-8	-15	-22	-29	-36	-43	-50	-57	-64	-71	-78	-84	-91
45	26	19	12	5	-2	-9	-16	-23	-30	-37	-44	-51	-58	-65	-72	-79	-86	-93
50	26	19	12	4	-3	-10	-17	-24	-31	-38	-45	-52	-60	-67	-74	-81	-88	-95
55	25	18	11	4	-3	-11	-18	-25	-32	-39	-46	-54	-61	-68	-75	-82	-89	-97
60	25	17	10	3	-4	-11	-19	-26	-33	-40	-48	-55	-62	-69	-76	-84	-91	-98

Frostbite Times ☐ 30 minutes ☐ 10 minutes ☐ 5 minutes

Wind Chill (°F) = 35.74 + 0.6215T - 35.75(V^{0.16}) + 0.4275T(V^{0.16})

Where T= Air Temperature (°F), V= Wind Speed (mph)

Effective 11/01/01

will be lost. I've included a wind chill factor chart supplied by the National Weather Service, but keep in mind that the chill temperatures listed pertain only to exposed human skin. To use the chart, locate the current temperature across the top and the current wind speed on the left hand side. The figure listed where the two columns intersect is the wind chill factor temperature.

Deer are warm-blooded mammals just like we are. As such, a combination of cold temperatures and wind would cause them to lose body heat faster than they would on cold days without any wind. But deer also have fur and a very minimal amount of exposed skin. To my knowledge no one has come up with a wind chill factor for mammal species other than humans, so we really cannot quantify as a temperature what the rate of heat loss would be for a healthy deer. Yes, animals do get frostbite and there are many sad documented cases of dogs and cats left outside to fend for themselves in biting cold, but they are not deer. Dogs and cats have exposed paw pads, and have a different kind of fur. So where does that leave us with deer and the matter of wind chill factors?

While deer can't calculate a wind chill factor, they do instinctively somehow know that it is detrimental to be exposed to a combination of very cold temperatures and high winds. On days when these conditions exist, I've found that they bed in areas sheltered from the wind near a food source. Watch for fresh tracks and sign in the snow pointing you in the direction of shelterbelts, cattails along swamps and marshes, ditches and the tree cover of forests.

In the chapter about wind I mentioned its three-dimensional aspect. Likewise, there is a three-dimensional aspect to temperature that the prudent hunter is wise to prepare for. This is especially true of hunters pursing deer in areas where mountains or hills may take them up and down a couple of thousand feet or more in elevation during the course of a day. Just like barometric pressure, temperature decreases with altitude. The rate of decrease depends on something called the lapse rate, and that has to do with moisture and instability of the air mass at a given location, but it will roughly be between 3 and 5 degrees for every thousand feet of altitude increase.

This is why I really recommend a layered approach to hunting clothing in mountainous terrain. If you're on a guided hunt, be sure to ask the guide how much of an elevation increase or decrease he expects to encounter on the day's hunt. You could easily find yourself in a situation where a

Tammy Nelsen dressed in layers to stay warm on her first-ever deer hunt. The day started out chilly, and the layers kept her comfortable long enough to wait for this unique "one-horned" whitetail to come within range of her .243 rifle. Photo by Mark Nelsen.

temperature change accompanying a change in elevation necessitates the addition or removal of a layer of clothing. For example, you could start out on a hunt around noon with a temperature of 35 degrees at the base camp with the intent of descending 3,000 feet to a valley floor where you'll await the herd coming down off the mountain to feed later in the day. Depending on the condition of the atmosphere, you could arrive at your ambush position and find the temperature to be 45-50. If the hunt takes you up 2,000 feet you'll find yourself in temperatures well below freezing instead of just above.

An exception to this increase and decrease of temperature depending on elevation is the presence of a temperature inversion. It's called an inversion because the usual state of the atmosphere is to cool with altitude, but there are conditions that can "invert" that state and result in a layer of stabilized or warmer temperatures above a pool of cooler air. In the winter months, approaching warm fronts attempting to sweep cooler air out of an area will create temperature inversions, but they can also take place in mountainous terrain on a much smaller scale that varies from valley to valley. In those cases a layer of milder air may establish itself between two mountains and it's called a thermal belt. Thermal belts are most pronounced during the nighttime hours and typically occupy the middle third of a mountain's slope between the peak and the valley floor. Inversions and thermal belts inhibit vertical movement of air. For that reason, deployment of scent lures and cover scents can be quite effective beneath the inversion layer. But thermal belts really don't have much of an impact on hunting, as they're stronger in the hours of darkness. However, knowing the elevation at which a thermal belt can typically be found might make for more comfortable sleeping by avoiding the significantly colder valley floor and mountain peak. In short, a thermal belt is a nice place for a spike camp or base camp if you can find enough flat space for one on the mountainside.

To summarize the impact of temperatures on deer and deer hunting, it is reasonable to conclude that deer inhabiting certain regions become acclimated to the temperatures that dominate those regions. Personal observations or information provided by state game management agencies can help determine what range of temperatures deer in a certain area are best adapted to. Temperatures warmer than those deer are accustomed to tend to make the animals sluggish and desirous of areas that offer cooling shade and water. Temperatures colder than those deer are accustomed to cause them to seek the most readily available food sources and sheltered bedding areas closest to them. My observations have led me to conclude that both whitetail deer and mule deer don't care much for temperatures higher than 80 degrees or lower than 25 degrees and their activity levels decrease when temperatures exceed both the high and low extremes of this temperature range. Activity levels increase when temperatures are in the middle of that range. Wind chill factors as we understand them do not affect deer in the same way that they do humans, but deer will avoid exposure to a combination of wind and very cold temperatures by seeking sheltered areas near food. Hunters need to remember that temperature does vary with altitude, and they need to be prepared for possible sudden changes that may be encountered for both comfort and safety reasons. Now that we have a better understanding of how deer respond to temperatures and wind, let's see what they do when stuff falls from the sky.

CHAPTER 6

The Sky is Falling

Rain, sleet, snow, hail and drizzle all have something in common. They are products of a process that in one way or another originated when the invisible water vapor that is constantly present in varying degrees in the air around us condensed into a visible water product and found its way back to the ground. As such, each is a form of precipitation and precipitation for deer hunters is sometimes good, and sometimes not so good. I don't want to dwell too long on the processes that form each specific kind of precipitation, so here is the condensed (pun intended) version.

Right now, inside or out, the air you're breathing contains water. You can't see it because it is in the form of invisible water vapor, but it's there. Relative humidity is expressed as a percentage referring to how much water is in the air around you compared to how much it could hold at the current temperature and pressure. If the relative humidity is 58%, that means the air contains 58% of the water it could before becoming saturated. When the relative humidity hits 100%, the invisible water vapor condenses into fine water droplets and becomes visible in the form of a cloud. In very simple terms, a cloud in contact with the ground is known as fog.

Many people struggle with understanding relative humidity and dewpoint. Relative humidity is a percentage. The dewpoint is the temperature to which air must be cooled in order for invisible water vapor to condense into

The author put water in a glass and then refrigerated it overnight. The next day he removed the glass and set it on a patio table. As the chilled water and glass cooled the outside air to the dewpoint temperature, water droplets began to condense on the exterior of the glass. This process of cooling air to the dewpoint temperature turns the invisible water vapor in the air into visible water and is the initial stage by which water vapor is turned to clouds and clouds eventually produce precipitation. Photo by author.

visible water. The closer together the air temperature and dewpoint temperature are, the closer the water vapor in the air is to condensation and therefore the higher the relative humidity is. When the temperature and dewpoint are the same, the air is saturated and the relative humidity is 100%. Perhaps an illustration will help.

Let's say on a hot and muggy day you go to your refrigerator and remove a cold glass of water. The temperature in your refrigerator is set at 40 degrees. As soon as the glass of water cooled to 40 degrees leaves the refrigerator, it begins to rapidly cool the air that the glass comes in contact with. Let us say the dewpoint temperature in your kitchen is 65 degrees. When the cold glass cools the air immediately in contact with it to 65 degrees, water will form on the outside surface of the glass. As more air comes in contact with the glass, there will soon be so much moisture on its surface that small drops of water will run down its sides and onto the coffee table, prompting you to retrieve a paper towel or a coaster before your wife sees you leaving water rings on wooden furniture.

In the same way, a front, upper level disturbance, the sun's heat, moist winds blowing into mountain ranges or other lifting forces in the atmosphere will begin to move air from ground level upward. If the air mass is unstable, lifting forces will be aided. If the air mass is stable, they will be suppressed. As I've already pointed out, air cools as it rises. When air from the surface rises and cools to the dewpoint temperature, its invisible water vapor condenses and becomes visible floating above the ground as a cloud. In a stable atmosphere, a few puffy clouds are as far as the process gets. But if the atmosphere is unstable, lifting forces continue and literally wring the moisture out of the

If the atmosphere is stable, the clouds will have a flat appearance to their tops and precipitation is unlikely (above). In an unstable atmosphere, the tops of clouds will show enhanced vertical development (below) and there's a much better chance of precipitation. Photos by author.

air. Water droplets in the clouds merge, or they bond to ice crystals in the clouds and freeze. This merging process is called coalescence. There will come a point when water drops or ice crystals become too large and heavy to remain aloft, so they fall to earth as rain or snowflakes.

All precipitation begins with the cooling, condensing and coalescing processes. Hail, sleet, and freezing rain create some unpleasant end results at ground level, but this is the way the show gets started. While you may find this interesting, you're probably wondering when we'll start talking about deer again, so here we go.

Deer respond to different forms of precipitation in different ways, just like you and I do. For most of us, a little fog or drizzle is gloomy and annoying but doesn't put an end to our usual routines. I've found the same to be true of deer. Moisture that accumulates on everything that fog and drizzle come in contact with may mean we'll have to strip the rifle down at the end of the day for a good cleaning and drying session, but it won't keep us from the hunt. Nor should it. I've harvested many deer feeding in the early morning mists. Remember that deer can meet part of their daily water requirements by ingesting moist plant matter, and if fog and drizzle are moistening the grasses, alfalfa

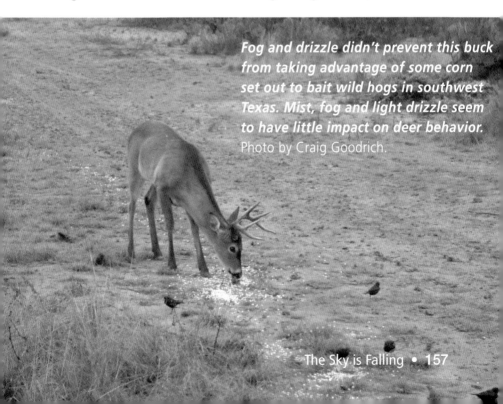

Fog and drizzle didn't prevent this buck from taking advantage of some corn set out to bait wild hogs in southwest Texas. Mist, fog and light drizzle seem to have little impact on deer behavior. Photo by Craig Goodrich.

leaves or corncobs in the field, they can eat and "drink" at the same time from the same source. Dew on food sources can also supplement a deer's daily water intake, but dew is not precipitation. It is water vapor that has condensed right onto the plant surface as that surface cooled to the dewpoint temperature. In my experience, fog resulting in visibility of a quarter mile or more, drizzle and light rain do not keep deer from their typical daily activities, but such weather does present the deer hunter with both challenge and opportunity.

In the chapter on pressure I referred to the excellent sound-transmitting properties of moisture in the air. I need to clarify that statement further because that is only true if the moisture present is suspended in the air and not making any noise itself. In a heavier drizzle, for instance, the sound of the drops falling on and through leaves can mask the footfall of an approaching hunter. A moist forest floor also has what I call "the carpeting effect" by making the sound of a hunter's steps more like walking on carpeting than on a linoleum kitchen floor with all the sticks, twigs and leaves on the ground. But great care must still be taken to close the distance with your quarry as quietly as possible, even if drizzle is falling hard enough to give you some covering noise should you snap a twig. However, if the foggy and drizzly morning is deadly quiet and still, deer will compensate for the reduction in vision defenses created by the weather by reacting very quickly to any sound or scent that could be perceived as a threat. I recently visited a natural science museum where a plastic cast set of ears replicating those of a mule deer was on display for visitors to experiment with. Yes, I looked ridiculous, but it was a fascinating exercise as I donned the pair of ears and listened. The shape of a deer's

Deer have excellent eyesight and hearing, but their primary sense is scent. A very large portion of a deer's brain is devoted to scent acquisition and analysis.

ear is ideally engineered for sound amplification. I had no meters or testing equipment but I would estimate that just by wearing those plastic ears, ambient noises in the museum were increased by at least 50%. What's more, angling the ears in a specific direction clearly "targeted" incoming sounds from that direction. It gave me even greater respect for a deer's sense of hearing, but as good as that is it is not their primary defense mechanism.

Deer possess excellent hearing and eyesight, but it is their sense of smell that reigns supreme when it comes to detecting what's in their environment. An amazingly large portion of a deer's skull and brain are devoted to scent detection and analysis. Deer hunters have to always remember that there are two ways humans transmit scent, and foggy mornings put a lot of favorable cards in a deer's hand.

Hunters produce human scent by introducing it into the air around them, and by leaving it on the trail behind them. Scent-blocking hunting garments are effective in controlling transmission of human scent into the air, but only to the extent that they cover the hunter. Hunting deer in a moist environment amplifies their already superior ability to smell you and demands maximum coverage in scent-blocking material. Your coat, pants, socks, boots, gloves, hat and facemask must all be able to mask your scent, and neglecting to cover any portion of your body only tips the odds in the deer's favor. Your Scent-Lok® coat won't do you much good if you're not wearing scent-blocking pants, and the coat and pants won't help you if your head and face are rolling human scent contained in water droplets from precipitation or sweat onto the shell of your coat. And don't stand around the camp stove while bacon and eggs are cooking for breakfast in your scent-blocking gear on a moist morning. You'll not only scare deer away with the smell of your breakfast when you do get around to hunting, but you could actually invite some bears or boars in your direction as well traipsing around the woods smelling like a Perkins Tremendous 12 Breakfast Platter. Regularly clean your scent-controlling clothing items according to the manufacturer's directions, and then keep them in an airtight container until you arrive at the hunting spot and change on-site. There may be some buddies who'll laugh at you, but it's you who'll be smiling if they get shutout and arrive back at the truck to see you sitting on the tailgate over a monster buck. So head-to-toe scent control is a great idea on misty mornings, but there's still the problem of the scent trail you leave behind you as you stalk or head to the stand.

A deer's nose is so sensitive that he'll not only know you've been by when he crosses your trail, but he'll know how long ago you were there and what direction you were heading. Odor-controlling boots and pants certainly are an asset, but your footwear will carry trace scents from every place you've worn it recently, and big old buck's don't get big or old by being dumb. If a trophy deer crosses your trail and gets a whiff of cow manure and fertilizer, he'll get to wondering how those scents got from a farm field a half mile down the road onto his rutting ground – especially if he hasn't seen any cattle or spreaders in the area. That's why a lot of hunters swear by cover scents on a drag cloth. But using cover scents incorrectly can be just as bad as not using any at all.

Nobody knows when the rut is on more than the deer do, and relying on mating-based cover scents before the rut begins or after the rut has ended will tip off any deer that something isn't right. If deer rut in your hunting area in November, you don't want to be using doe-estrous or buck-rut cover scents on a late September bowhunt as you walk to your stand. I may not be pleasing to be around, but I like using skunk cover scent. That's because I know the area I hunt is loaded with skunks, a deer isn't going to want to sniff around it too long, and a big buck won't think too hard about coming across skunk smell. I know some hunters like a food-based cover scent, but if you are going to use one for the first time in an area, you'll be better off making sure that the food smell you'll be giving off is from a food source in that area. Deer understand that corn doesn't grow well in orchards and you won't find many acorns in a wheat field. I can't emphasize enough how important it is to understand that moist environments, whether they're caused by fog, drizzle or even dew, keep any scent given off by a hunter lingering in an area for hours. This is knowledge that can make or break a hunt. Used wisely, scent-blocking agents, attractants and trail-covering scents can really increase the chances for success.

Fog can and does mess up a deer's visual defense ability, but it can also mess up the hunter on offense. Optics are one area of hunting gear that I've learned not to skimp on after seeing too many hunters get frustrated with fogged-up scopes and binoculars. If you've taken everything else into account and can close the distance on a deer in fog slowly enough, he may sense you but not be able to figure out what you are if he can't hear or smell you and your outline is broken up. Really good optics can help you see him better than he can see you, especially if the situation allows you to approach in fog with low-hanging sun at your back. The dispersion of bright light behind you as morning mists lift will further confuse a deer, even though he may see you. That gives you one advantage, but as I mentioned

before we all have a responsibility to know where our bullet will go before we pull the trigger. I've hunted in fog several times, but never taken a shot unless I could see a good backstop behind the deer. For the well-prepared and safety-conscious hunter, going after deer in fog or drizzle is a challenge fairly easy to overcome. But what works well and is important in a moist environment may not be so critical in a wet one.

People used to ask me what the difference is between light rain and drizzle. Rather than get into a technical discussion about drop size and formation, the simple "hunter's answer" is that drizzle gets you wet without you knowing it until you are, and you'll know it's raining when you hear and feel actual drops hitting you and things around you. Where fog and drizzle may tip the odds slightly in favor of the deer, moderate rain can favor the hunter by creating some cover sound and washing human-caused odors away. That doesn't mean you throw out the rulebook on sound and scent stealth, but it does give you a wider margin of error.

I've harvested many deer in fog or drizzle, relatively few in moderate rain, and none in heavy rain. As I mentioned before, light to moderate rain can give a hunter in a cornfield or forest good cover sound. That's a good thing because deer tend to bed down in sheltered areas when the skies open up and the only way you can hunt them is to jump them from their beds. This is also the case when moderate to heavy sleet and snow are falling. The deer will bed and you will have to go to them.

When you stalk in hopes of jumping a deer in precipitation, keep in mind what I mentioned in the chapter about fronts. Deer normally flee away from the hunter and then turn to run into the wind. That way the deer's nose can sense what's ahead, it's 300+ degree vision and rotating earcups will also tell the deer what's ahead, to the sides and whether or not you're following behind. But in heavy precipitation of any kind, a deer may flee away from you initially into the wind, but then turn quickly to run with or parallel to the wind instead of against it. To do otherwise would slap precipitation into the deer's highly sensitive sight, smell and sound organs, a situation most deer find intolerable for more than a short-distance sprint.

A tactic that has proven to be successful for me on two hunts in wind-driven sleet could be effective for other groups of two or three hunters. In both cases, the wind was blowing hard from the northwest and I suspected that the

Blacktail deer hunters in the Pacific Northwest often experience rain or snow, depending on the elevation. Snow can accumulate quickly in the highest elevations, but at the same time precipitation may be falling as rain lower down. Dedicated blacktail hunters clearly need to be ready for anything. Photo by Mark Boardman.

deer would be holding tight in the cover of the river bottom that borders the property I hunt on the north and east. The sleet wasn't heavy enough to call the hunt off and visibility was more than a mile, but it was annoying and stung my face as I trudged northward along a two-track dirt trail on the west side of the property. Stealth wasn't a concern as I walked into the gusting wind. I'm selective about who I hunt with on my honey hole north of the Black Hills, and I usually try to give my guest a chance to fill his or her tag first. The tactic was identical on both of these hunts, and I positioned my companion shooter about a third of a mile south of the north tree line and about 200 yards west of the east tree line at the base of a lonely big oak in the

Persistence and preparedness are key to a successful blacktail hunt given the often sudden and dramatic weather changes found in the environment of the species. Mark Boardman has been hunting blacktails since he was a youth, and is pictured here with a full-bodied buck he harvested in thick cover in Washington. Photo courtesy of Mark Boardman.

middle of the field. A group of whitetails was right where I thought they'd be on the north tree line in both cases. In one situation the deer broke cover when I jumped them as I turned east along the river in the trees, and the deer headed south, away from me and in the opposite direction of the wind-driven precipitation. They nearly ran over my guest! The shot was a close one and filling that antlerless whitetail tag was easy. On the second occasion, the deer fled their beds running east instead of south, but turned south along the east tree line where the river also turned in that direction rather than attempt a crossing. Refusing to run into the wind and sleet, the deer turned toward my guest's ambush position and a buck fell to his .30-06 bullet a few minutes later.

I mentioned earlier that deer seem to adapt to certain environments, and while the hunting-in-rain tactics I've outlined have been very effective on whitetail and mule deer, the blacktail deer of the Pacific Northwest and Alaska may be an exception to some of my rules. During the rainy season from October into March in that part of the country, any blacktail deer that waited for dry weather to feed would starve. Strong storms move in off the west coast and lash the area from northern California into British Columbia with driving rains and wind that can last for days. If sufficient cold air is present, heavy wet snow will blanket mountaintops and drive blacktails downhill.

I interviewed a skilled blacktail hunter who swears by hunting them in weather that would have a Texas whitetail or North Dakota mulie bedded down and waiting things out. But a deer has to eat to survive, and hunters who set up overlooking clear-cut openings in the dense Northwest forests or who watch saddles leading into them while it is raining can apparently do quite well. I have to take his word for it because I've never hunted blacktails personally, but the reasoning seems sound. While other deer species may be reluctant to venture into the open when heavy precipitation is falling, the blacktail deer will do so when it's time to feed and leave their beds. I suspect this may be the case because whitetails and mule deer in other parts of the country "know" that incessant rain or snow for more than a day is unlikely, but blacktails "know" it can rain or snow for several days in a row and have adjusted their behavior accordingly.

Deer don't seem to mind being out in light snow as much as they do in moderate to heavy rain or sleet, and I have seen herds quite active when it was snowing lightly. When heavy snow moves in, however, hunting becomes a real challenge. In 30 years I can only recall harvesting two deer in what I would call a heavy-snow situation, and the difficulties presented by those hunts will likely cause me to wait until the snow stops the next time I'm faced with similar conditions. The challenges presented by reduced visibility, locating the deer, getting the deer back to my vehicle and the treacherous drive home all gave me second thoughts afterwards.

In light snow deer behave much as they do in drizzle or light rain, but when the flakes are falling large and fast they will bed down and wait it out. I'm amazed at how deer seem to be able to sense whether or not a coming snow event will be a big deal to them or not. In mountainous terrain, deer will often migrate downhill to be closer to food sources just before a heavy snow, and on the plains they will often move toward farm fields or wildlife management areas for the same reason. They will feed aggressively up until the start

This incredible photograph provides clear evidence of two key facts. First, the buck is bedded down in cover during a heavy snow event. Second, the amount of snow accumulation on the deer's antlers is nearly identical to the amount of accumulation on branches adjacent to him. This would only be possible if the deer bedded down just as the snow event was beginning. Photo by Denver Bryan.

of the heavy snow event, and then settle down somewhere until it is over. If you do a search for deer in snow photos on the Internet and scroll through the hundreds of images, you'll notice that on many there is an accumulation of snow on the animals that are bedded. In some pictures you may even notice that the accumulated amount of snow on the deer is comparable to the amount accumulated on adjacent tree branches. In order for that situation to exist, the deer would have had to bed down about the time that the heavy snow began.

To bare human skin, snow is cold and wet. But snow is also an excellent insulator for warm-blooded animals able to get around the problem of contact with its cold moisture, and a deer's winter coat seems to be able to help it do that. As snowflakes accumulate, their crystalline structures interlock with a good deal of air space between the flakes. This dead air space between flakes can work much in the same way that high-loft down does in winter outerwear. If you take a class in outdoor survival skills you're likely to be taught how to build a snow shelter with a cold-air sink and vent. Deer can't tell us, but I suspect that they don't mind a bit of a snow blanket now and then, and they don't seem to be in a hurry to shake it off when they get up. In fact, deer don't seem to be in much of a hurry at all when the snow is accumulating at a decent rate, and a bit of snow on the back and rack can help those big bucks blend in better with the branches, too.

I mentioned killing two deer in heavy snow. Both were taken in a recently harvested cornfield where they had bedded down between the rows of what was left of the stalks and were absolutely motionless. The snow was 6-8" deep and visibility varied from 75-125 yards. The harvesting of the animals was amazingly easy in that we basically walked up to within 30 yards of them, stalking into the wind. Just as cottontails sometimes hunker down in hopes that a hunter won't notice them and pass them by, so too those deer just lay there as we approached even though I was certain they'd seen us. Eventually they stood up and, being sure of our background, we shot them. The easy part was over.

Walking in snow is good aerobic exercise. Dragging a deer back to a vehicle is good aerobic exercise. Walking in snow while dragging a deer behind you is extreme exercise and certainly not for those who have physical challenges or limitations. Heavy snow can make downed deer that would otherwise be more accessible by vehicle inaccessible, and then you have a real chore ahead. Wheeled game carts are great when you have relatively solid ground to use them on, but they don't do well in deep snow or mud. The best way I know of to reduce the stress on the hunter during a game retrieval in heavy snow is to use a game sled. They retail for around $30, and that is a cheap investment compared to the chiropractor or cardiologist bills you may face if you try to do without one. But there is a downside, literally, to game sleds. You have to be very careful when you find yourself going downhill or across a hillside. A deer carcass on a sled isn't exactly lightweight cargo and you don't want it swinging around

you only to drag you face first through the flakes down an embankment. "Deerboarding" is not desirable winter recreation. Snow retrievals have to be taken slowly and routes planned carefully to avoid what at best could be a comical and humiliating story your buddies will never let you live down, or at worst could be a situation resulting in serious injury.

Some hunters actually prefer to hunt when there's a fresh-fallen snow because they say it makes deer easier to track. Yes, fresh snow does show where animals have passed by since the snow ended, but much of the talk of tracking deer in snow among the old timers I hunted with when I was young did not pertain to locating deer. They wanted snow on the ground to help find their deer once the animal had been hit. There's no doubt that a crimson blood trail stands out well on a bright white background and will help them do that, but the longest blood trail I've ever had to follow during a rifle deer season was about

The author harvested this South Dakota whitetail buck the day after 6"-8" of snow fell. The buck was on its way out of the Black Hills to lower elevations to feed on the hay of a local farmer.* Photo by Karen Carlson.

15-ft. long. During my three decades of big-game hunting with a long gun I've shot deer with 12-gauge slugs, a .243, a 7mm Remington magnum, a .30-06, a .45-70 and a .50-caliber muzzleloader. Good ammunition and accurate shot placement from any of these firearms should require little in the way of tracking once a deer is hit. While I do understand things don't always turn out as we'd like, every hunter's goal should be to drop game where it stands. Archery hunting is a bit different given the dynamics of how an arrow kills, and snow cover is certainly a huge benefit to the bowhunter. Regardless of the weapon used, the hunter has an ethical responsibility to do all he or she can to make any blood trail as short as possible. And when I'm finished field-dressing a deer in snow I will kick snow over the gut pile and residual bloody areas to "clean it up." That way, any snowmobiler, snowshoer, or cross-country skier that happens to pass by won't see a bloody mess that could contribute to anti-hunting sentiments.

A fresh snowfall can tell you quite a bit about the activity going on in the deer's environment since the last flakes fell. Reading tracks in snow is fun, interesting and educational. You're apt to encounter footprints left by anything from mice to mountain lions, depending where you hunt. When I'm out hunting the day after a snow and encounter a good set of deer tracks heading into cover such as a marsh or a cluster of brush, I'll often follow it back a ways to see where the deer had been before it entered cover. You may be able to locate a food source, and that knowledge could come in handy later if you haven't filled your tag yet. If you do this, be sure to walk a few feet to the side of the deer's trail and not over it. Drag your feet a bit with each step to mess up the human foot outline as much as possible. I don't want to be accused of giving deer more intelligence than they have, but I think they're somehow able to discern which kinds of tracks predators (including humans) leave whether by sight, scent or instinct. Wolves, coyotes, cougars and other consumers of venison will walk on top of a deer's tracks, using their noses to pick up details about the animal they're tracking and they won't have the trouble pursuing into cover that you and I do. If you track off to the side a ways using a cover scent or scent-proof boots and pants, the backtracking buck will know something was around, but you may be able to convince him that it wasn't a threat. Don't succumb to the temptation to follow the deer tracks into the cover right away. The deer likely knows the layout of that patch of cover better than you do and has his escape routes in mind. Once you enter it, he can wait for you to get into

Large hailstones, such as this baseball-sized example, can be composed of smaller hailstones fused together. A strike on the head from such a hailstone could result serious injury or even death for a human or animal. Photo courtesy of the NOAA Photo Library, National Severe Storms Laboratory/U.S. Department of Commerce. Public domain.

the thick stuff and then bolt from it, leaving you with no shot because you can't maneuver your gun around in the cover. Also keep in mind that tracks made in the snow degrade rather quickly in sunshine unless the temperature is well below freezing, but in very cold weather the snow tends to be powdery and the tracks aren't as well defined. Temperatures from 25 to 30 degrees are what I find best for reading track information. With temperatures relatively close to the freezing mark you can usually get a well-defined edge on the tracks as they imprint better with higher definition of detail. The crisper the image of the track edges, the fresher the track is.

If you know the size of the cover area a deer recently entered and the wind conditions permit your doing so, see if you can back off, go around it in a direction that keeps you downwind, and check to see if the deer has left it. There's no sense in staking out a hiding spot that's unoccupied, but at least you'll know where one good hiding spot is. Every such place you can mark on your GPS has the potential for a filled tag later on.

The final kind of precipitation I need to cover is hail. Hail and sleet are two different "species" of frozen precipitation and completely unrelated when it comes to how they form. Hail is produced by thunderstorms that are most likely to be encountered on early-season bowhunts or youth hunts. Hunting in thunderstorms is dangerous for a variety of reasons that I'll discuss in the next chapter, but hail is precipitation so I'll cover it here.

Hail in the United States ranges from pea-sized all the way up to more than a foot in circumference. The National Weather Service has established a threshold of .75" diameter or greater for classifying a thunderstorm as "severe," and hail kills game animals. While open-country upland game birds such as sharptail grouse and pheasants are most vulnerable to hail, once hailstones reach 1.75" or greater in diameter they are capable of bringing serious injury or even death to animals and humans. Big-game animals of the open plains such as antelope and mule deer are most at risk, but mule deer don't have the reluctance to crossing fences that many antelope do. The photos supplied by Todd Nordeen, a District Wildlife Manager for the Nebraska Game and Parks Commission show in graphic detail what can happen when animals are caught in the open by hail. He told me the story behind the pictures.

"Myself and Aaron Fellows were conducting our annual vehicle, pronghorn doe/fawn survey in Sioux County, northwest of Crawford. Shortly into the survey, we observed one pronghorn, approximately 300 yards off the road. It exhibited odd behavior for a pronghorn by just standing there with its head down. It was on public land (Ogallala National Grasslands) so we decided to take a closer look. As we ventured closer we were surprised to see several pronghorn dead in the area. In all there were 23 dead pronghorn. There were also dead insects and rodents in the area. The vegetation had also been stripped and beat down. It became apparent that a hailstorm had gone through the night before. We did find out later that golfball- to baseball-size hail was reported in that area with high winds. Some antelope were obviously injured and died due to blunt force trauma to the head from the hail but it also appeared that the storm created panic in the herd causing many of them to slam into the fence at high speed."

Todd Nordeen, Nebraska Game and Parks Commission

Photos courtesy of
Todd Nordeen of the
Nebraska Game and
Parks Commission.
Used by permission.

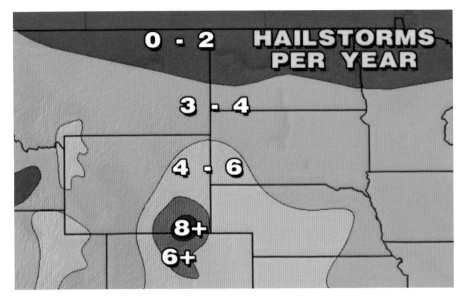

Geographic distribution of hailstorms. Graphic by author.

While Florida has more thunderstorms per year than any other state, the part of the country that sees the most hailstorms per year is a zone along the front range of the Colorado Rockies from north to Gillette, Wyoming and east to South Dakota's Badlands, then south across the high plains of Nebraska and Kansas. A smaller area from Denver, Colorado, north through Cheyenne, Wyoming, averages between six and eight hailstorms per year.

A shelf cloud, like the one above, is often seen on the leading edge of a storm with large hail and damaging wind. Photo by Randee Peterson. Copyrighted by www.blackhillsweather.com. Used by permission.

Mammatus clouds are an indication of extreme turbulence in a thunderstorm, and a warning sign that the storm may contain large hail. Photo by author.

Deer will not remain out in the open in hail, and neither should deer hunters. Deer also will be on extra-high alert immediately following a bad hailstorm. When strong thunderstorms approach, both the deer and deer hunter should seek shelter. If you don't have a weather-alert feature on your GPS or FRS/GRMS radio unit, darkening skies and the first rumbles of thunder are your cue to get to shelter. Often times, mammatus clouds will precede severe thunderstorms and the sight of them approaching is another warning to get to safe shelter. By the time you see a shelf cloud heading your way, you may have less than 10 minutes to get to cover. If you see a shelf cloud and feel a sudden drop in temperature, find the closest and lowest cover you can find and get ready to hunker down until the storm passes, but watch for any hint of rising water in your shelter ditch or draw. Be sure not to present a target for lightning by getting below surrounding terrain features and vegetation. If hail starts to fall, put your pack over your head and neck as you sit with your knees against your chest, elbows on your knees and hands holding the pack in place. If the hail gets big you'll take a beating, but will likely survive with your head, neck and chest covered.

No matter what kind of precipitation you encounter on your hunt, it will be a benefit to you to know how long and how hard the rain, thunderstorm or snow event will be ahead of time. In spite of all the jokes made about weather presenters, today's professional meteorologists have computer models and tools that have made short-term weather prediction more accurate than it has been at any other time in history. Your most reliable source for precipitation information will be a NOAA weather radio receiver, and the good news is that the amount of real estate covered by National Weather Service transmitters across the nation has increased dramatically and there are now more than 950 of them. Like cell phones, you'll have areas without reception, especially when you're deep in the wilderness. But if you hunt farms and ranches in the vicinity of small towns, chances are that you'll be able to receive information on one of the seven channels NOAA transmits on. While NOAA weather radios used to be desktop models, today there are lightweight portable receivers no bigger than a calculator. Several makers of GPS units and FRS/GMRS radios now have NOAA receivers built into them. NOAA weather-alert radios will sound a warning tone when severe weather bulletins are issued for an area. Yes, such a tone would alert every animal within a quarter mile to your presence if you have that feature activated, but it could also save your life. There are even models that silently display icons or text alerts to warn you when dangerous weather is approaching.

And while I'm on the topic, don't ever believe anyone who tells you that a hunter doesn't need to be concerned about weather-related hazards.

A National Weather Service Doppler radar transmitting tower.

CHAPTER 7

When Weather Turns On You

I remember my first impressions of the Alaskan wilderness. Few places I have ever been on this earth are as beautiful. Yet the entire time I was hunting caribou north of the Brooks Range there was an unmistakable message being communicated by the land around me. Amidst the wonder of the scenic vistas was the message, "I can kill you any time I want to." That is the message of nature. We are her guests and we play by her rules or else. It doesn't matter if you're stalking Cape buffalo in South Africa, hunting ducks in Louisiana bayou country, pursuing pheasants in South Dakota, stalking blacktails in the Pacific Northwest, or moving in to close the distance on a moose in Maine, each region has dangers that hunters must be ready for.

I was at a meteorology conference some years ago when someone put forth the idea that most people killed or injured in weather-related incidents were in part responsible for their own deaths and injuries. It was an idea that, on first impression, seemed unnecessarily cold-hearted until the 50 some meteorologists attending began to discuss it. If you've lost a loved one to a weather-related disaster,

Though beautiful to behold, the mountains of Alaska's Brooks Range can be a treacherous and dangerous place where weather changes are sometimes rapid and extreme. No matter where a big-game hunter ventures, it is wise to research potential hazards that could be encountered beforehand. Photo by author.

please don't toss this book into a blender until you hear me out. Yes, weather-related fatalities can seem completely random, but if you can detach yourself from the emotion of the tragedy and take a hard and honest look at the statistics pertaining to causes of death or injury, there is a very clear common element in many cases and it's "human error." Examples would include those that perish attempting to cross flooded roadways in a vehicle, unaware that as little as a foot of fast-moving water can sweep some vehicles off the road and downstream. Then there are those that fail to heed winter storm or blizzard warnings, become trapped and never reach the destination they valued more than their lives. Some choose to live in tornado prone regions without any storm shelter nearby, betting their lives on the odds against a twister's direct hit or on their ability to outrun an approaching storm. Still others disregard evacuation orders when a major storm is bearing down on them until it's too late and the roads are either cut off or too clogged with traffic to make evacuation feasible. Rather than cruelly question the intelligence of people whose lives nature has claimed in severe weather events, I think it is fairer to say they died because they underestimated or misunderstood the forces of nature they were dealing with.

For the hunter, understanding the threats to life and health while hunting is critical. Many of the incident reports available to the public concerning hunter injuries and fatalities in the field focus on the causes we're familiar with. Most hunters that fail to return from the field wind up with their deaths falling into the very broad category of "accident." You'll read about firearm-related accidents, accidents involving falls from treestands, slip-and-fall injuries and so forth. What is more difficult to ascertain from these reports is the role, if any, that weather might have played. Did someone fall from a treestand because the steps were icy or snow covered? Did treacherous footing in rain-soaked mud play a part in a slip-and-fall accident? Was a hunter attempting to cross a stream swollen from overnight rains when he was swept downstream? Did a fall through ice thinned by a recent mild spell result in a drowning? Were slick roads to blame for the hunting vehicle leaving the road on the way to the hunt? Did grass dried by drought touch the pickup's catalytic converter and start the grass fire? Was a hunter's heart attack brought on by overexertion as he trudged through deep snow or exhaustion from heat and dehydration? You can see how weather might play a subtle, yet significant role in the fate of hunters in the field.

Most of the hunters I know are well prepared for their adventure, and many carry some of the same items I do. My daypack contains a military first aid kit, a liter of water (sometimes two), dry socks, a 2-ft. x 2-ft. blaze orange fabric square, two FRS/GRMS radios, my GPS, a cell phone (and I don't have a subscription), six pairs of surgical gloves, a pair of insulated waterproof gloves, a small saw, a butane lighter, duct tape, a pen, some paper, extra keys to my vehicle, snacks and a good flashlight. I also usually carry a sweatshirt, an extra orange cap and some paper towels. That may seem like a whole bunch of stuff, but the heaviest item is the water. On long wilderness trips I'll just throw in my little water purification system and get my water on the hunt, as I need it. In my vehicle I keep an axe, fire extinguisher, larger saw, tool box, sleeping bag, extra food, dry footwear and 12-volt adapter for the cell phone.

Before we get into the reasons for all this stuff and tie them into deer hunting, there are a few things that need to be said about technology. Many people purchase so-called "emergency cell phones" that are intended to call 911 only. Makers of these phones say that no subscription fee or sign-up fee is needed, and in that they are correct. My family rebelled against technology by doing away with our cell phone subscription two years ago, but we still keep the old phones around. Why? Because the FCC requires cellular phone service providers to put ANY 911 call through to the nearest emergency dispatch office whether that phone has an active subscription or not. So if you still have an old

FRS/GMRS radios can be very handy tools for hunters in areas where their use is permitted, but as is the case with any electronic device, don't depend on them exclusively to get you out of trouble. I highly recommend models that have a NOAA Weather Alert feature or are at least capable of receiving broadcasts from NOAA weather radio stations such as this Midland model. Photo by author.

phone lying around from an old provider, charge it up and toss it in your pack. A 911 call for help must be put through, PROVIDED SERVICE IS AVAILABLE in the area you're calling from. That's the key point. Don't rely on that cell phone to get you out of trouble if you're in the middle of wilderness where there is no cellular service signal.

The same goes for FRS/GMRS radios. Use of these radios to communicate the locations of game to other hunters is permitted in some states, and illegal in others. But most states do permit general communication between hunters so long as game isn't mentioned in the conversation. These handy devices are great for telling buddies you're running

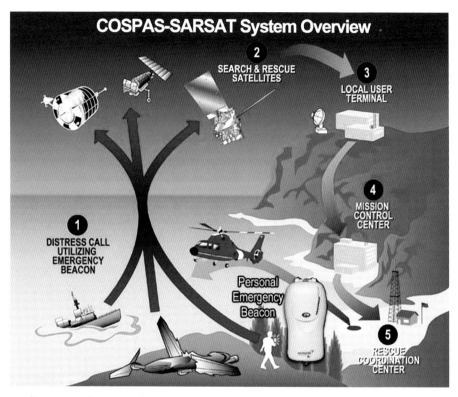

A diagram showing how Personal Locator Beacons (also known as Personal Emergency Beacons) work. Graphic courtesy of the National Oceanic and Atmospheric Administration. Used by permission.

late for a rendezvous, informing them of an accident or getting help if you're lost if your radio can reach someone able to give you directions. Some models of FRS/GMRS radios boast ranges in excess of 16 miles, but keep in mind that for most that means line-of-sight and requires a special license from the FCC. Terrain features can easily block your signal. A conservation officer in Colorado told me that his agency monitors FRS/GMRS communications to find, fine and jail hunters that break the rules that state has against using the radios to transmit the location of game, but that also means a distress call MIGHT be picked up if an officer was listening to the right channel in the right place. Like the cell phone, the handheld two-way radio COULD be a life-saving tool, but cannot be counted on as one.

In recent years we've seen the introduction of the Personal Locator Beacon, or PLB. At $500 to $700 these are expensive electronic insurance policies, but they can and do save lives. The advantage to the PLB is that is works anywhere. Should a PLB-equipped hunter become trapped, hopelessly lost or injured, he or she can activate the device. Within a minute, the PLB starts sending a signal to U.S. and Russian satellites in orbit that is then retransmitted back to a federal facility affiliated with the National Oceanic and Atmospheric Administration (NOAA) in Maryland. The emergency signal is processed to determine the exact location of the transmitter and steps are taken to find out if it's a false alarm or genuine emergency. Once the determination is made that an emergency signal may be valid, search-and-rescue teams are dispatched to the location of the signal's origin.

This system has proved to be very effective and saved many lives, but it is not without drawbacks. PLB owners must register their unit before using it and its code is on file with the government so that those responding to it will know who you are. If your PLB is stolen it's important to notify authorities of that fact, and it is equally important to do so if you sell yours or buy a used one. Also, because there is no voice communication, first responders will have no idea as to the nature of your distress and response time can be 45 minutes or longer. If you're seriously injured it's important after activating the PLB that you use a pen and paper to start writing whatever you can about the situation. That way, if you lose consciousness the first responders will have some idea as to what they're dealing with. Even a cryptic message such as "Snake bite left ankle," or "Chest pain. Suspect heart attack," will be of great use to those responding to your call for help. But also keep in mind that there may be conditions that keep rescuers from getting to you right away such as darkness if they can't see you, or foul weather. Activating a bright flashlight and aiming it upwards if it's dark may help in the first instance, but if you're stuck in a sudden mountain blizzard you may be on your own for a while.

Because you can't rely on James Bond gadgetry to get you out of a bind, the best defense the hunter has is not to get into one in the first place. That means being prepared and having enough common sense to realize when it's time to call off the hunt and get back to the vehicle or camp. Every hunter is different with different thresholds of comfort when it comes to what is and isn't safe pertaining to weather. No ethical hunter will ever compel a companion to continue a hunt if that person is concerned about impending weather-related danger. No deer is worth losing your gear, your vehicle or your life over, and trips to the hospital ER aren't exactly cheap these days, especially if they involve aerial transport to the facility. Yes, search-

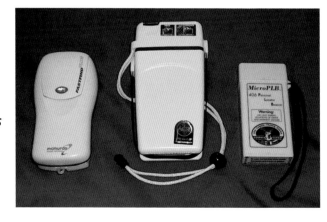

What some models of PLB look like.
Photo courtesy of NOAA. Used by permission

and-rescue people are paid to do a job, but you may find them a bit terse if they discover that poor judgment or stubbornness is what got you into trouble in the first place. Some of them may not appreciate having to risk their lives to save yours when that's the case.

So what kinds of things should hunters be on the lookout for that could get them into trouble with rapidly changing weather? After all, it's not always easy to get The Weather Channel in a spike camp on a mountain or a remote lodge in Southern woodlands with no electricity. Forecast accuracy deteriorates about 10% for every 24 hours after issuance, so the forecast you heard three days ago on TV will only have a 65%-70% chance of being accurate if you haven't had access to a new one since that time.

Two important things to monitor on a hunt are the winds speed and direction along with barometric pressure tendency. In the chapters dealing with those subjects, I talked about the strength of wind being related to pressure change and how air flows from the high pressure-area toward the low-pressure center. Fall deer seasons correspond with a volatile time when the atmosphere in North America is in transition from summer to winter, and that is a time when there can be extreme changes in the weather over a very short period. These changes will usually manifest themselves in one of two ways, depending on what part of the country you are hunting in. The sudden change could come in the form of thunderstorms, some of which might contain very heavy rain, hail, lightning, damaging straight-line winds or even tornadoes. Hunters in the southern and eastern parts of the nation are most likely to encounter strong thunderstorms during hunting season, though there is also a short thunderstorm activity increase in the northern plains during September bow seasons. The bigger threat in the western mountains and northern states is the very dangerous rain-turning-to-snow situation accompanied by high winds and rapidly falling temperatures as was the case with the Armistice Day storm of 1940. In the Pacific Northwest, fall marks the onset of the rainy season with the threat of storms that produce high winds, lengthy periods of rain (or snow in the higher elevations), flash floods and mudslides. In each of these regions, strong winds from the northeast to south quadrant of the compass accompanied by rapidly dropping barometric pressure should put hunters on "yellow alert" for potentially dangerous weather. When clouds start to increase, lower and darken, the time you have to get to shelter may be short. When winds become southwest to northwest off the ocean as the storm center moves east, more heavy precipitation is likely as moist ocean air is lifted over the coastal mountains and Cascades. If you wait until the first drops or flakes fall, you may have waited too long.

Thunderstorms produce a variety of threats. Lightning usually kills more people each year than tornadoes and ranks second on the list of weather-related killers. To ladies it will come as no surprise that the majority of lightning-strike victims in the United States are males involved in outdoor recreation, and most are struck on weekend afternoons. In fact, more than 80% of lightning strike victims are male, but death has been instantaneous in only about 20% of the cases recorded. For reasons science has yet to explain, men are also more likely than women to survive a lightning strike, but the majority of lightning strike survivors develop other significant medical problems afterwards.

Lightning kills and injures dozens of American outdoor enthusiasts every year. It's interesting to note that the majority of strike victims are males engaged in outdoor activities on weekend afternoons.
Photo copyright 2004 by Eric A. Helgeson, www.skewphoto.com. Used by permission.

Here are some interesting facts about lightning that you may not be aware of. The average diameter of a lightning bolt is about the same as that of a pen. The bolts look much bigger and are visible from such great distances because of the incredible amount of energy they contain. Lightning bolts may contain 1,000,000 volts of electricity and are more than five times hotter than the surface of the sun. Lightning can hit a person or object 10 miles away from the parent thunderstorm that produced the bolt and the sun can even be shining overhead, hence the phrase "bolt out of the blue." If you can hear thunder, you are in range of the storm's lightning and will usually not be out of range until

20 minutes after the last thunder is heard. The worst place to seek shelter from a thunderstorm is under a tall tree as lightning tends to strike the tallest object in the strike zone, and in an open field YOU are the tallest object in the strike zone. Lighting may give you just enough warning before it hits to respond in a manner that will get your bell rung, but could avoid a direct hit. If you should feel your hair start to stand on end, the electrical charge is building on or near you. Drop to your knees immediately, put your head between them (this isn't a joke) and kneel in as small a ball as you can make yourself. This presents the strike from above with the smallest profile target. If you drop and spread eagle on the ground, you're increasing your body's target area from above. If you should be with someone who is struck, understand that they carry no residual electrical charge (in spite of what you may have seen in some science fiction movies), and immediate administration of CPR is often successful in reviving a victim. Even if it is not, continue CPR until paramedics arrive.

For deer hunters, the safest place to be when thunder and lightning are imminent is in a building or vehicle. A very bad place to be is in a deer stand with a powder-coated steel frame overlooking a field, and no, any rubber in your boots will not protect you. If you can't get to a vehicle or building, run into the thickest GROUP OF TREES you can get into and sit down on the ground between some of the shorter ones. Turn off all electrical gear you may have with you, including radios, GPS units, cell phones and music players as there is some anecdotal evidence to suggest that the presence of activated personal electronics could increase your chances of being hit. Do not return to your deer stand until at least 20 minutes after the last

A huge rotating wall cloud just west of Sidney, Nebraska, in June 2005 produced a large tornado that ripped up many trees just east of the town of Potter. Hunters are unlikely to encounter tornadoes during fall deer seasons in the northern and western states, but they remain a threat year-round in the South. The distinctive rotating wall cloud is a block-shaped formation protruding out the bottom of a severe thunderstorm. If you should happen to see one approaching, take cover immediately. Rain may obscure your view of the tornado, as it does in this picture. Photo by author.

thunder has stopped and there appears to be no possibility of additional storms.

Occasionally, thunderstorms will produce dangerous straight-line winds and tornadoes. More tornadoes take place in the United States than in any other country on earth with an average of about 1,000 per year. National Weather Service statistics report an average of 80 deaths and 1,500 injuries caused by tornadoes annually in America. When you consider how many tornadoes take place, it's a wonder that more people aren't killed or hurt.

The reason for this is the impressive improvements that have been made by the NWS over the last two decades in getting warnings out to the public before a tornado hits.

Spring and early summer are the peak months for tornadoes, but they can happen during any month of the year depending on where you hunt. There is little risk of tornadoes in the Northern Plains, Pacific Northwest, Rockies and Northeast during fall deer seasons, but hunters from Texas eastward along the Gulf Coast to the Mid-Atlantic States need to be ready for them year-round.

Since a severe thunderstorm must be present for a tornado to form, a deer hunter would hopefully already

The same tornadic storm as seen from the other side of the wall cloud. From this angle the large tornado funnel is not obscured by rain and is clearly in contact with the ground. Photo by Michael Morgan. Used by permission.

Still another picture of the same tornado. It formed the characteristic funnel formation several times, then seemed to disappear only to reappear over and over again. The clue that this tornado is still in contact with the ground is the small debris and dust swirl near the ground. Even as this picture was taken, the tornado was causing damage to the farm compound silhouetted in the photo without any apparent connection to the parent thunderstorm. Photo by Michael Morgan. Used by permission.

be in a safe shelter because heavy rain and hail often accompany or precede the tornado in a tornadic storm. But should you find yourself caught in the open trying to wait out a storm and see a tornado approaching, get as low as you can go. Tornadic winds are weakest within 6-ft. of the ground, so find a place below surrounding terrain such as a ditch, hole or other depression in the ground. Most people hurt and killed in tornadoes meet their end as a result of flying debris. It helps to remember that tornadoes are invisible. What you see in the form of a funnel is a mixture of sand, dirt, rain and debris rotating around the tornado core. The tornado is a giant, violent, fast-moving cross between a belt sander and a blender. You don't ever want to come in contact with one. Tornadoes can kill wildlife, but deer are very fast runners with heightened senses that can usually help them escape the danger before it gets to them. Though deadly, tornadoes rank among the least likely weather threats a deer hunter will encounter.

Floods kill more people than any other weather-related hazard each year in the United States, more than tornadoes and hurricanes combined. And about half of those fatalities involve people attempting to cross fast-flowing water. In spite of pleas from weathercasters and the National Weather Service not to do so, people persist in crossing flooded areas and meet their doom in one of two ways. Either they misjudge the strength of the current and are swept downstream, or the murkiness of flowing floodwaters conceals underwater dangers. A well-built male hunter can be swept downstream by as little as 8" of fast-moving current. Lightweight vehicles such as ATVs, UTVs motorcycles and small cars can be swept off the road by as little as 12" of fast-flowing water, and 18"-deep water can float some trucks and SUVs away. You might think that you're vehicle is too heavy to float. Does it weigh less than a yacht? Big and heavy objects float easily if the right physical conditions are present. For cars and trucks, it's a matter of buoyancy and applied force against the side of the vehicle. When a vehicle is crossing flowing water, all it takes is water deep enough to reach the running boards or bottoms of the doors to suddenly amplify the force pushing it downstream many times over. The more vehicle cross-section exposed to the current, the greater the push. So having a bigger vehicle in such a situation doesn't always offer much of an advantage.

The Rapid City, South Dakota, flash flood of June 1972 demonstrated how easily vehicles can be moved downstream by floodwaters. This photo was taken after waters had receded and shows cars bunched and stacked like toys where the current left them. Photo courtesy of the NOAA National Weather Service Collection. Public domain.

For deer hunters the threats posed by flooding rains are especially dangerous, and not just for the reasons I've already outlined. Because we tend to drive on two-track country trails, backcountry dirt roads and mountain switchbacks, the places we drive aren't always in the best shape to start with. Many of them have culverts interspersed under the trail periodically, and heavy runoff is notorious for washing out roads around culverts. This happens as branches, rocks and other debris block the upstream entrance to the culvert, forcing the water up and over the dirt road that is then swiftly eroded away. To a hunter approaching such a washout there is the illusion created that the water is only a few inches deep over the road when the reality is that there is no road left under the water, only a culvert. Such a situation is a terrible accident waiting to happen. If there is even the remotest possibility that you could be wrong about the depth of the water ahead of you, do not attempt to cross it.

Every hunter must take flash flood watches and warnings seriously, but hunters in hilly or mountainous terrain are especially vulnerable to this threat. The earliest settlers discovered that the best way to get around in the mountains was to travel through the valleys and passes. Modern engineers thought that was a good idea too, so most of the ways in and out of good deer country are between the hills and mountains. On my first hunt in the Black Hills, a veteran of many seasons told me, "If you get lost, just keep heading downhill until you reach a road or water and then keep following them downhill. Eventually you'll find your way out." I did get lost that first day, I did as I was told, and other hunters in the party found me sitting beside a road heading downhill taking a breather. But water also flows downhill, and when it does so in large amounts, people die.

Big Thompson Canyon on July 31, 1976. It was Colorado's Centennial Weekend and the canyon was full of people in campers, tents and motels. A wall of water from a stalled thunderstorm extinguished nearly 140 lives, injured nearly 90 other people and caused millions of dollars of damage.

Rapid City, South Dakota, on June 9, 1972. A freak storm dumped more than a foot of rain on the Black Hills and the water raced down Rapid Creek, breeching Canyon Lake Dam. The wall of water that raced through town that night killed nearly 240 people and injured approximately 3,000.

These are among the worst flash floods in U.S. history, but most of us only hear about the other flood related

On June 1, 1997, a thunderstorm produced flash flooding south of Norris, South Dakota. At the height of the flooding, water seemed to be flowing across this country road and at first appearance looked rather shallow. But below the current the road had washed away on both sides of the culvert, creating a deathtrap for any motorist that would have attempted to cross. Photo courtesy of the Rapid City, South Dakota National Weather Service Office. Used by permission.

deaths from local news outlets because it happens to a person here, and two people there at a time. Ask anyone who has been through a flash flood and they're likely to tell you two things: They had no idea that water could rise and move in so quickly, and they had no idea how powerful a surge of rushing water could be.

The National Weather Service, a branch of NOAA, is responsible for the issuance of severe weather watches and warnings. A watch means that the event for which the watch is issued is possible in the watch area during the time frame indicated. Its purpose is to give those in the watch area time to prepare before the actual threat materializes. Over the years, the National Weather Service has seen a significant increase in the number of watches that actually need to have warnings issued within them later. In other words, the weather gurus have gotten pretty good at letting you know ahead of time when you'll get hit. A severe weather warning means that the threat for which the warning is issued is taking place or imminent. When a warning is issued, your response should be to take immediate action to protect your life.

If you are hunting in an area under a flash flood watch you have two options. You can call off the hunt for the day to get your vehicle or camp to safer, higher ground, or you can risk continuing but limiting your hunting to the highest terrain in your hunting area. Bear in mind that a hunt in heavy rain is a low-percentage-of-success hunt anyway in most parts of the country. If a flash flood warning is issued for your area, your only option is to get to high ground immediately. If your vehicle is parked in a warned valley, consider it lost and run uphill as fast as you can. If you're lucky, your rig may still be there when the warning expires. If your not, at least you'll be alive but have been taught a very expensive lesson.

Another threat from flash flooding and heavy rain is mudslides and landslides. Areas most prone to these sudden land movements are steep hillsides with sparse, dry or thin vegetation, steep terrain, unstable geological features and areas recently burned by wildfires. With no deep-rooted vegetation to hold the soil in place, it quickly becomes saturated and if conditions are right, the land can suddenly break apart and slump downward. Most mudslides are smaller scale events and not a lot of people are killed by them compared with other weather-related disasters. For big-game hunters in remote areas, the biggest threat they pose is to block roads and trails, trapping the hunters so they can't get home or back to

Areas recently burned by forest fires are very susceptible to mudslides and water runoff until significant vegetation is reestablished. Hillsides, such as the one pictured at the south edge of Chadron State College property, can green up quickly after a fire and eventually evolve into prime grazing areas for deer and elk. The risk of mudslides and flash floods remains, however, until plants with root systems capable of holding soil in place grow again. The area pictured was burned in 2006 during the Spotted Tail fire with the photo taken in the spring of 2007. Photo by author.

camp. On more than one occasion I've read of hunters trapped in remote areas by mudslides or flooded roadways only to have the rain turn to snow. If you are ever trapped in an area because mudslides have blocked your way out, abandon any notion of trying to dig through the mud and clear a path. More mud uphill will just slide into areas you might clear and bury you, you'll expend precious energy you may need to survive, and the last thing you want to be when you know you have a long stretch ahead in the wilderness before help arrives is tired, wet, muddy and cold. While these sudden land movements can take place anywhere, the U.S. Geological Survey Web site contains map information of areas most susceptible to landslides and mudslides. In the lower 48 states, the areas of greatest risk lie along the Appalachian Mountains (especially Pennsylvania and West Virginia), in Colorado's Central Rockies and the Pacific Northwest.

Hypothermia is a major killer of wilderness lovers. Campers, hikers, climbers and anglers have all fallen to this insidious weapon in nature's arsenal, and I suspect that more hunters have fallen prey to hypothermia than any other weather-related hazard. Information from the Mayo

Heavy, wet snow and rain-turning-to-snow situations pose several dangers to hunters. Tree limbs can snap off, and entire trees can fall over. Wet snow is more difficult to walk in and also tends to be very slippery. Hunters forced to deal with a wet snow situation need to focus on staying dry to avoid hypothermia, and must also use great care when walking or driving.

Clinic suggests that nearly 700 Americans lose their lives to hypothermia each year. It results when a person's body is no longer able to produce or retain enough heat to sustain normal metabolic functions and maintain body temperature. To put it more simply, their body temperature starts to drop well below normal. Humans are considered to be in a hypothermic state if body temperature drops to 95 degrees or lower. You'll note that is only 3 degrees below normal.

One serious misconception that some might have is that hypothermia presents a danger only when weather is extremely cold. What they fail to realize is that the unprepared hunter is just as susceptible to hypothermia when temperatures are in the 50s as he or she is in blowing snow with temperatures in the teens and subzero wind chill factors. In fact, of the nearly 1,000 cases of hypothermia in the U.S. each year, the majority occur when the temperature is between 30 and 55 degrees. Getting soaked by an unexpected cold rain shower in your treestand when it's 52 degrees can be just as dangerous as getting soaked with sweat while dragging a deer through deep snow when the temperature is 20 degrees. In other words, every hunter needs to be prepared to deal with hypothermia in any cool-weather condition.

The onset of hypothermia is gradual, but can then rapidly progress through stages until the situation becomes critical. The primary manner in which deer hunters become exposed to hypothermia is by getting wet from sweat, precipitation or accidental exposure to water when the ambient temperature of the environment is well below normal body temperature. Even the slightest of breezes can accelerate hypothermia by increasing the rate at which the body loses heat to the environment.

Goose bumps and shivering accompanied by cold toes and fingers are often the first indication that you're in trouble, and such symptoms are not to be taken lightly. They are your body's way of telling you that you need to warm up fast. Failure to heed these warning signals will bring on the next set of symptoms that include clumsiness, a loss of coordination, difficulty performing simple tasks, such as unloading a firearm, and difficulty in concentration. By the time these symptoms show up the need for action is critical and immediate and there's no time to lose. Get the afflicted person warmed up. Experts recommend removing him or her immediately from the elements, getting the victim out of wet clothing and into dry clothes or a sleeping bag, and administering warm liquids and foods. In the event that a heated vehicle or shelter cannot be reached, find a place out of the wind and precipitation where a fire can be built to warm the victim and dry their wet clothing. Under no circumstances should a person experiencing hypothermia be given beverages containing alcohol. Such beverages create the illusion of warming, but in reality further inhibit the body's ability to retain heat. Do not rub the victim. Doing so not only doesn't help, but also could enhance risk of cardiac arrest in certain situations. It's also important to remember to warm a person from the core outward, even if they insist only their legs and arms are cold. If a person in otherwise good health responds to the mentioned first aid procedures favorably, the prospects for recovery are usually good.

Once a hunter becomes listless, denies being in distress, shivers uncontrollably, becomes argumentative, has difficulty speaking and walking, seems confused or disoriented, and doesn't respond favorably to first aid, it's time for emergency medial evacuation to the nearest hospital. Continue the hypothermia first aid procedures to the best of your ability, but seek medical attention without delay. In extreme circumstances it may be necessary to share body heat and the most effective means of doing so is through skin-to-skin contact with the both of you wrapped in a dry sleeping bag or blankets. Understand how rapidly hypothermia can set in. Progression through the stages of symptoms in some circumstances can be measured in minutes and reach a critical, life-threatening situation in as little as a quarter hour in certain conditions.

The good news is that hypothermia is very preventable, and your best defense is keeping abreast of the latest weather conditions and donning the proper hunting clothing before you venture into the fields and forests. Wearing a moisture-wicking and fast-drying base layer

The author favors waterproof kangaroo leather boots with 200-gram insulation for cool-weather upland game, deer and antelope hunts.
Photo by Frank Ross.

next to your skin can go a very long way toward protecting yourself. There are a number of such clothing products available, and they work by moving perspiration moisture away from your skin for evaporation. Evaporation is a cooling process and having it take place away from the skin can reduce the rate of body cooling.

A waterproof, yet breathable outer garment could be another life-saving investment. Today's hunter has many choices in outerwear that incorporate materials that block wind and moisture from penetrating from the outside, but still allow perspiration vapor to escape from the inside. The term "breathable" is often used to describe such garments, and they will serve to further transport perspiration moisture away from your skin. And by far, the best approach to hunting attire is to use layers of garments that have the features I've identified. You want a moisture-wicking base layer, an insulating layer, and a breathable yet waterproof and windproof outer layer. Outdoor clothing retailers sell sometimes two or more of these layered components as "systems" garments. As the hunt progresses, you can always shed unneeded layers and stow them in your pack. I've found it far better to be over prepared than unprepared.

Finally, don't forget the accessories. The most critical area to cover to retain body heat is also the one I see many hunters uncover first, and that's the head. A significant amount of body heat can be lost through the head, face and neck, and keeping these areas covered will go far toward prevention of hypothermia. In cold weather, mittens are more effective than gloves when it comes to keeping fingers warm, but I use something called a glomitt on cold-weather hunts. It offers the warmth of a mitten, but the finger section folds back to allow me to shoot, load or perform brief tasks demanding greater dexterity by temporarily exposing my fingertips. And insulated, waterproof, breathable boots are a must. How much insulation is needed in a boot? That really varies from hunter to hunter according to personal comfort levels, but one way of calculating it that works for me is to think in terms of needing 200-gram insulation for every 10 degrees below 40. So I'll wear my 200-gram boots if I'm hunting in 30-40 degree weather, my 400-gram boots in 20-30 degree weather and so on. For hunts in temperatures above 40 degrees I go with my waterproof uninsulated boots with wool socks and keep an extra pair of socks in my pack.

The winter storm is the deer hunter's nemesis. The weather that precedes it offers conditions that make for excellent hunting, but to tarry too long on the hunt when a winter storm is bearing down is to tempt fate with what could turn into a life-or-death struggle. For more than two decades I was a professional broadcast meteorologist and during that time I experienced almost every kind of severe weather a person can encounter in North America. I am

Blizzards often result in the closure of roads and can strand hunters for days. Whiteout conditions just east of this exit on Interstate 90 in western South Dakota prompted the closure of the state's main east-west travel artery. Photo courtesy of KEVN Black Hills FOX News. Used by permission.

also a storm chaser and weather photographer to this day. Yet in all of my weather-related experiences and encounters over the years there has been only one time that I have known fear, the kind of fear that makes a man's knees weak and renders him unable to speak even after arriving at safety. That fear came the night in January 1997 that I stupidly decided to take on a South Dakota blizzard in my 4x4 pickup, and it is not a mistake I shall ever make again.

For reason's I've already outlined, the days and hours right before a big storm hits seem to generate a spike in deer activity. That's what makes those times great for deer hunters. But winter storms take on a personality of their own and each brings weather conditions that have prompted some in the weather business to name them according to their origins and track. These names include the Alberta Clipper, the Nor'easter, the Colorado Low and the Panhandle Hooker. I've never heard anyone come up with a name for the storms that move off the ocean and into the Pacific Northwest so I'll just reference them here as Pacific storms.

Working from east to west, the Nor'easter is a winter storm that begins as a strong low-pressure center in the Southeast, and then tracks northeast along the coast up into the Maritime Provinces of Canada. For the Nor'easter to occur, the northern jet stream usually dips deep into the U.S. east of the Rockies, bottoms out along the Gulf States, and then curves sharply northeast east of the Appalachians. As a strong low tracks northeast along the jet stream, its circulation feeds moisture off the Atlantic and throws it into the cold Canadian air entrenched between the Rockies and Appalachians. When conditions are right, snow from these storms can be measured in feet. It is also usually very heavy, large-flaked wet snow with relatively high moisture content accompanied by strong winds. For Eastern deer hunters, the threats posed by the Nor'easter include rapid snow accumulation that can strand hunters for days if they don't get out of the woods ahead of the storm, and cold, wet conditions ripe for causing hypothermia in those unprepared. As these storms can shut down travel from the mountains eastward, hunters must be cautious to keep informed and plan to be well on the way back home before the first flakes fall. Deer will seek whatever shelter they can find, and snow may be so deep after a Nor'easter that they have difficulty moving or finding food. As the heaviest snow will usually fall in the highest elevations, deer may sense the weather change and move to lower elevations before the brunt of the storm begins. Clever hunters will have planned for this and be in position to take deer coming down from the high country ahead of the storm. Once the storm has left the area and travel is again safe, deer will likely be found on or near farms where food is easier to access. Hunters may be able to secure permission from landowners to harvest deer feeding on precious hay and cattle feed who would be grateful to see some deer removed from their property. My advice to eastern hunters would be to avoid danger best by working known approaches down from the high country preceding the storm, make sure you monitor changing weather conditions, get home before the brunt of the storm hits, and then head out again a full day or two after the storm to look for deer hanging around farmland.

The Panhandle Hooker is named because it tends to result from low pressure that crossed southern California and the Desert Southwest only to reform and strengthen in the vicinity of the Texas Panhandle. The northern jet stream is usually positioned diving southeast out of British Columbia into the Southwest, curving east into northern Texas, and then taking a sharp left back north across the Central Plains up into the Great Lakes. It's fed by moisture off the Gulf of Mexico and is probably the most dreaded of the five kinds of winter storms I've mentioned. The reason for this is that the Panhandle Hooker draws warm and moist air northward with it, resulting in unseasonably mild weather from south to northeast of the storm center. Even in mid-winter, strong thunderstorms with severe weather can develop along the storm's trailing cold front and then

Lowering and darkening clouds before the onset of winter precipitatio.
Photo by author.

march eastward. Depending on the position of the storm and precise weather conditions, the Panhandle Hooker can bring devastating ice storms from the northern part of the Gulf States through the Central Plains and then slam those same areas with snow on top of the ice to make travel impossible. Power lines snap, tree branches break and traffic accidents abound. For the hunter there is added danger.

One of the things hunters from the Central Plains to the Great Lakes need to be concerned about is a rain-changing-to-snow situation. This was what happened during the Armistice Day storm of 1940 and what ultimately killed so many hunters. The Panhandle Hooker can deceive by fooling deer hunters into thinking the dire weather predictions were wrong if the day dawns much warmer than average. Here's a rule that deer hunters will do well to remember: Beware mild mornings when big change is predicted. On such a day, anytime your hunt begins with temperatures above freezing there will be the chance that the precipitation, when it comes, could start as rain. If you're not ready for that you'll get soaked and be at very high risk of hypothermia when the cold front arrives, temperatures drop like a rock, and the rain turns to snow. As is the case with other approaching storms, deer will be active until the cloud deck lowers and precipitation begins. Safety demands that deer hunters not wait too long before heading back to shelter, and make sure the shelter is stocked with provisions for three days. Panhandle Hookers can be slow moving storms with precipitation from start to finish lasting up to 48 hours, and some of that could come in the form of a full-blown blizzard. The National Weather Service defines blizzard conditions as sustained winds of 35 mph or more accompanied by falling or blowing snow that reduces visibility to ¼ mile or less for a period of 3 hours or more. It's important to note that blizzard conditions can exist at ground level even with blue sky overhead. In these cases the storm center has passed far enough from the area for precipitation to have stopped, but strong pressure differences between the low pressure leaving the area and high pressure moving in create such strong winds that the fresh-fallen snow is blown around to the extent that visibility is ¼ mile or less. This is called a "ground blizzard" and is just as dangerous for travelers as a blizzard with snow falling from the sky. When a Panhandle Hooker finally leaves the area, it's usually followed by a blast of very cold air from Canada. Deer will be hungry when storm conditions end, but the heavy snows will likely make it hard for them to find natural food sources. Watch for them to move into agricultural areas after the storm, especially on the first clear, calm and very cold mornings and evenings after the storm has ended. When the cold snap ends and snow cover thins, they'll venture further from agricultural interests in the course of their wanderings, but won't venture too far from them again until the snow melts.

The Colorado Low is, in many respects, similar to the Panhandle Hooker only it forms farther north and tends to track east a bit before angling up toward the Great Lakes. This kind of storm also tends to move a little bit faster and, generally speaking, the faster a storm moves the less snow it deposits on an area. There are exceptions to every rule, but usually a potent Colorado low will deposit a strip of heavy snow in the 8"-14" range with locally higher amounts in the mountains and across Nebraska, the eastern

Dakotas, Iowa, Minnesota and Wisconsin before heading into Canada. Severe thunderstorms and some potential for ice storms can exist south and east of the storm center. Colorado lows that hook more sharply to the north can bring very heavy snows to the Black Hills, western Dakotas, eastern Montana, eastern Wyoming and the Nebraska Panhandle. Because of their faster-moving nature and the shorter time between their formation and full-blown winter storm conditions developing, hunters in the high plains may not have much time to take advantage of high levels of deer activity prior to the storm's arrival. This is where the value of a good extended weather forecast comes in. If a hunter is always looking days ahead and sees snow predicted for a couple of days four or five days out, a visit to the Web site of the nearest National Weather Service Forecast Office (NWSFO) will provide opportunity to read the scientific

On March 13-14, 2002 a Colorado Low winter storm dumped more than a foot of snow from northwest Nebraska into central South Dakota. This is a photograph of the region taken the day after the storm. Spring storms in this part of the country often produce heavy snow with high moisture content that is badly needed to replenish water systems, but heavy wet snow is also very hard on wildlife and livestock. The dark area on seen on the South Dakota/Wyoming border is the pine-covered Black Hills region. Also visible are the Pine Ridge area of northwest Nebraska, the Missouri River through central South Dakota and the Minnesota River in Minnesota. Photo courtesy of NOAA and the Rapid City, South Dakota National Weather Service Office.

weather forecast discussion. There will be many terms unfamiliar to those not accustomed to reading them, but you'll get a general idea of the kind of storm predicted for the area. Such information can be valuable in determining whether to take a couple of vacation days to hunt in advance of the storm or to postpone plans until after it has passed. Like the Panhandle Hooker, the Colorado Low is followed by a cold snap and a period of high winds that can produce blizzard conditions, but because these storms tend to keep moving, the duration of such conditions tends to be shorter. Once things settle down, look for deer to be out and active very quickly. Those in higher terrain will have moved lower just prior to the storm. They'll be browsing for food wherever they can find it, including near farms and ranches, but also on any exposed ground on hillsides, in creek draws, and in river bottoms where the winds may have blown snow clear of vegetation.

The Alberta Clipper gets its name from the fast old clipper ships that used to trade goods across the seas in the 19th century. That's because these storms are so fast. Known for producing relatively small amounts of snow compared to the other winter storms (3"-6"), occasionally a storm of this type can generate extreme amounts of snow when conditions are right. It is also the kind of storm capable of generating huge snow accumulations on the upwind slopes of large hills and mountain ranges in its path. The Alberta Clipper is renowned for escorting frigid Arctic air into the northern and central states. It can also cause brief blizzard or whiteout conditions. A whiteout is a situation where snow and blowing snow is so intense that a person literally cannot distinguish sky from ground or what direction they are traveling. The amount of lead-time a hunter has before an Alberta Clipper arrives can be short, and if one is expected to cross your hunting ground during deer season, be ready with your best cold-weather hunting gear. The cold temperatures associated with the Alberta Clipper mean the snowflakes tend to be lighter and fluffier, more prone to blowing around. After the storm, the bitter air will make stalking difficult, as this is the kind of storm that makes snow squeak underfoot when you walk and lashes you with fierce wind chill factors. Deer will move to lower-elevation woodlands, creek bottoms and draws to wait out the storm. The combination of wind and light nature of the snow will also mean some areas will have impressive drifts, while others will be blown clear. The nice thing about this kind of storm is its brevity. Only on rare occasions will the snow last more than a day, unless you're hunting the windward side of mountainous terrain. If you only have a few days to hunt, you're likely not to be shut in the whole time by an Alberta Clipper. Just make sure you pack your Thermos and heavy long underwear.

This sheep became disoriented and died where it lay last in a severe blizzard on January 9-10, 1997, that killed tens of thousands of livestock in the Dakotas. Many game animals and birds, especially pronghorn antelope, were also killed during the storm across the region. Snowdrifts as deep as 18 ft. were reported and wind chill factors in open areas dipped to –70 degrees. In the days that followed the storm, surviving deer raided the hay reserves of farmers and ranchers in the region who were desperately trying to get precious feed to stranded cattle. Photo courtesy of KEVN Black Hills FOX News. Used by permission.

Pacific storms can last for days on end. They'll lash coastal areas and the mountains inland with howling winds and bring large amounts of wet snow to the higher elevations with rain in the valleys. Snowfall from the Sierra Nevadas to the mountains of British Columbia can be measured in feet from a single storm event, and that's why the deer will move to lower elevations beforehand. Even then, persistent cold rain will demand the best insulated rainwear a hunter has at his or her disposal and the risk of hypothermia is again high for anyone unprepared. Travel on muddy back roads can be treacherous and the threat of mudslides very real. Often the breaks between these kinds of storms are brief, so hunters will be wise to pursue deer whenever nature gives them opportunity during the season, but also to be ever mindful of rapidly changing conditions. An excellent emergency plan and survival kit are essential when hunting this region after the rainy season has begun.

There is yet another kind of snow situation that really cannot be classified as a storm, but it still produces very heavy snow in certain parts of the country. It's called the lake-effect snow and is generally associated with the Great Lakes region during what would be the later hunting seasons. Lake-effect snow happens when cold Canadian air well below freezing moves over the still-open-water of the Great Lakes and deposits large quantities of snow from the downwind shore extending several miles inland. These snow squalls are fed by the temperature differential between the open water and air moving overhead, and they obtain their moisture from the open water. This kind of snow can last for days and poses potential problems primarily for deer hunters on the downwind shores of Lake Superior, Lake Ontario, Lake Erie and (in Canada) Lake

Huron. This kind of snow has also been associated with Utah's Great Salt Lake, and occasionally with other large bodies of inland waters when very cold air blows across them before they freeze. Lake effect snows cease when there's a change in wind direction or the body of water responsible freezes over.

From one extreme to the other we go, because hunters generally don't drink enough. Lest I be misinterpreted, I'm referring to water and the problem of dehydration. I have never had hypothermia, but I have had heat exhaustion and I highly recommend against it. There are two kinds of heat disorders hunters need to be aware of, and those are heat exhaustion and heat stroke (known in medical circles as hyperthermia – opposite of hypothermia).

Symptoms of heat exhaustion include heavy sweating,

Thirst, fatigue, excessive perspiration and the onset of a headache are ways your body tells you that you need water. These are initial symptoms of dehydration and should be taken seriously. Rest in a shady spot and sip water until you feel better. If symptoms do not subside, seek medical attention. Photo by author.

increased pulse and eventually a pounding headache. Then come the nausea and heaving. Left unchecked, heat exhaustion can lead to heat stroke. That's where the victim stops sweating, body temperature increases to dangerous levels; pulse and respiration increase followed by unconsciousness.

According to the Nebraska Hunter Education Student Manual, first aid for heat exhaustion involves getting the victim cool and re-hydrated, but don't let them drink too fast. Remove excess clothing and get the victim into shade. Lie them down with their feet slightly elevated. If there's a stream or lake close by, soak an article of clothing in it and gently dab the victim or fan them with some of the clothing you've removed. Have the person sip cold water. If no improvement is noticed after a half hour or so, get the victim to a hospital. If you come across someone you suspect is suffering from heat stroke, immediate live-saving action is needed. Call or send someone for help if possible. Keep the victim's head and shoulders slightly elevated above his or her heart. Remove excess clothing, but leave the baselayer on and moisten it with water if you have enough nearby. Fan the victim until help arrives.

You may think heat exhaustion can't ever happen to you, but when temperatures are in the 70s and even 80s during early seasons you'd be surprised how easy it is to get dehydrated, and dehydration is step No. 1 toward heat exhaustion. I went online and did a water requirement calculation for a 200-lb. hunter walking with moderate exertion levels for 30 minutes to and from a treestand. The calculator indicated that for optimal body efficiency, that hunter would have to drink 148-oz. of water that day (a gallon is 128 oz.). The problem is that water is heavy.

Staying hydrated is an essential part of hunter safety. Pause as often as needed for water breaks. Photo by author.

A gallon weighs 8 lbs. and most hunters, myself included, can't carry the amount of water needed as we hike around all day. I've hunted a lot of years and have yet to see a deer hunter lugging a gallon jug through the woods, but staying hydrated is important so how can it be done?

My field pack has holders for two 1-liter bottles of water (for all practical purposes, a liter equals a quart). That's nearly a half gallon weighing 4 lbs. that sits on my hips so as not to strain my back. I drink a bottle of water at the start of my hunt before I leave my truck with the two liters in my pack. I have half a liter of water with a mid-morning snack and drink the rest when I eat my lunch. If the afternoon is really warm I'll use the other liter on my pack for two water breaks. At the end of the hunt, I drink yet another bottle back at the truck and I'm good enough for the day. Some hunters carry coffee or pop in a pack and that's fine, but it doesn't count toward staying hydrated. In fact, caffeine accelerates dehydration so extra water would be needed to make up the difference. Sport drinks can count toward staying hydrated as they contain essential minerals and electrolytes your body needs.

And don't think that the temperature has to be hot in order for a hunter to become dehydrated. Anytime that exertion to the point of perspiration takes place, water in the body must be replenished. Climbing through rough terrain, trudging through heavy snow, or dragging a deer a considerable distance in any weather can sap precious moisture from a hunter's body.

There is yet another danger that hunters need to be very aware of, especially in the western states. A good chunk of the U.S. from the High Plains through the Rockies and into the Southwest has experienced several years of drought. I used to be part of a wildland firefighting team as a fire meteorologist. My job was to predict what a fire was going to do based on the meteorological conditions at the time and those predicted in the hours ahead. I've seen what a fire can do up close. Many state game agencies are justifiably concerned for the safety of habitat and hunters in light of tinder dry conditions, and long-range forecasts suggest that at least some of the West is likely to remain in a drought situation for years to come.

Over the years I've come to learn and respect just how easy it is for a fire to get started, and how fast a fire can get out of control. Sadly, it only takes a moment of neglect for a hunter to start a fire that could consume thousands of acres of valuable habitat. I once had access to some of the best pheasant-hunting ground in the world until a careless hunter in another party dropped his cigarette butt onto some dry grass. As the sun set that day you could see the smoke from that fire more than 10 miles away. Another way hunters accidentally start fires is by parking off the side of the road where dry grass can come in contact with the hot catalytic converter under a truck or car, or by driving off-road in an area where the same thing can happen. Wildfires can start from campfires left with embers glowing or be the result of a mistake involving a camp stove. Please understand that fire is a threat to you, your gear, the game you hunt and the land you hunt on.

If you should find yourself out hunting and see a wildfire start or approach, leave the area immediately and call for help. Never try to flee uphill away from a wildfire. I've seen flames outrun brush trucks, so they can sure outrun you. Fire tends to move uphill and with the wind the fastest. Your best way out is to run away at a right angle to the direction the fire is spreading if you can't run in the opposite direction of the fire.

There is much that has already been written about outdoor survival techniques, and I see no reason to review the importance of knowing first aid, how to build a shelter, how to build a fire, how to forage for food and collect drinkable water. When it comes to handling emergencies in remote areas the most basic thing for the big-game hunter to realize is that ignorance and panic kill, while knowledge, common sense and remaining calm save lives. You will not always be able to predict the kind of hazards you could encounter, but understanding weather and weather-related threats can go a long way toward helping you be prepared if the weather turns on you.

"Red at night is a sailor's delight" Photo copyrighted by Eric Helgeson, www.skewphoto.com. Used by permission.

CHAPTER 8

Weather Proverbs: Grandma's Wisdom or Folly?

Long before high-tech weather tools such as Doppler radar, weather satellites, sophisticated sensors and complex weather computers, people still attempted to predict the weather and how it would change. The jet stream wasn't discovered until aircraft that were developed during World War II became capable of flying high enough to encounter it. Weather fronts weren't called "fronts" until the term was introduced early in the last century to describe air masses doing battle. Luke Howard, an English pharmacist in the early 1800s, developed our modern system of cloud classification. Two of our nation's founding fathers were fascinated by the study of weather. Benjamin Franklin's weather experiments are very well known, and Thomas Jefferson purchased a barometer in Philadelphia on July 5, 1776, when he was in town for the signing of the Declaration of Independence. The study of weather goes back even further. The ancient Greek Aristotle wrote a book called "Meteorologica" in an attempt to explain not only weather, but also other theories about earth sciences around 350 B.C., and early attempts to unravel the mysteries of atmospheric science even older than that have been found by archeologists studying ancient Chinese and the Babylonians. From the time of Earth's earliest civilizations to the present day, learned men and women have put a single question forward. How can we better understand what the weather is going to do in the short- and long-term future?

For most of humanity's history, the only real means available for predicting weather was to observe nature, observe weather, and then draw conclusions that connected certain natural events with certain kinds of weather. In time, these cause-and-effect relationships manifested themselves in the form of weather sayings and proverbs passed down through the generations. Modern science now gives us the chance to validate or discredit these sayings, and hunters can be well served by knowing which are true and why. So let's take a look at a few weather proverbs and see if hunters might be able to use them, or if they even should.

A red sunset can be a sign of nice weather the following day.
Photo by author.

"Red at night is a sailor's delight!" This one's been around at least since the time of Christ. You can look up Matthew 16:2-3 in the Bible and see Jesus himself quoting a variation of it. It is a fairly reliable weather predictor for some very scientific reasons. In the mid-latitudes of the Northern Hemisphere weather systems generally move from west to east, and high atmospheric pressure is associated with fair weather. From an earlier chapter we know that air sinks under the influence of high pressure. This causes dust, pollen, pollution and other fine particles so tiny we may not even be aware of their presence to become trapped in the lower levels of the atmosphere. As the sun rises and sets, the amount of atmosphere its rays must pass through to reach your eyes is at its greatest. The tiny suspended particles in the air filter out the shorter wavelengths of the color spectrum through a process called scattering, and the longer light wavelengths that appear to us as hues of red and orange are the ones that make it through. It's logical to conclude, in the majority of cases, that a brilliant red sunset is the result of high pressure to the west and the following

Just as a defined halo around the moon can mean precipitation is on the way, the absence of such a halo and a very crisp and clear moonrise can be a sign that weather will remain nice on the following day. Here, the moon rises clear over Badlands National Park. Photo copyright by Eric A. Helgeson at www.skewphoto. com. Used by permission.

morning should at least dawn with fair weather conditions. A bright red sunrise may indicate the high-pressure center is shifting to the east and could mean barometric pressure will be lowering in advance of an approaching storm.

"A halo around the sun or moon, means rain or snow are coming soon." Ice crystals or high, thin cirrus clouds in the upper atmosphere cause the halo effect around prominent celestial bodies. This type of cloud may indicate that a weather system or warm front is approaching, but don't take "soon" too literally. The weather-producing front or system may still be quite a ways off and precipitation may not start for another 12-18 hours or longer. If you get up in the night and see the halo effect, chances are a sunrise hunt can go on as planned, but it's a clue that the next day might bring rapidly changing weather conditions and you'll need to be ready.

"The aching of a broken bone makes the coming of rain known." This is one of many variations on the theme that old injuries and arthritis will flair up with aches before a storm. Because cells in scar tissue expand and contract at a different rate than that of healthy tissue, the saying tends to be reliable when barometric pressure is falling at a pretty good rate. That means that low pressure and potentially stormy weather are on the way.

"Look for rain or snow when the crow flies low." There are several wordings of this proverb that may include such things as geese honking and insects flying or biting, but we now understand the reason behind them. Birds and insects seem to be very sensitive to atmospheric pressure changes and adjust their flight altitudes accordingly. The higher the atmospheric pressure, the nicer the weather and the higher you'll see birds and insects flying. As pressure drops, winged creatures tend to fly lower and falling pressure indicates a storm center or front is on the way.

"Flowers smell nicer before a rain." Air that is higher in relative humidity tends to carry scent better, and increased humidity coupled with falling barometric pressure is a good indicator that precipitation is on the way. As I mentioned earlier, lowering atmospheric pressure also can release gasses trapped under the waters of marshes and swamps. A less delicate way of putting this proverb might be, "When everything stinks, the weather might too."

"When smoke descends, good weather ends." We covered this a bit in the chapter on barometric pressure, and it tends to be true as long as there is relatively little wind around the

The fragrance of flowers is more pronounced when relative humidity increases. Moist air carries scents more efficiently than dry air. As barometric pressure falls in advance of a storm, humidity often increases along with cloud cover and eventually surface winds. All scents, not just pleasant ones, are usually enhanced prior to the onset of precipitation. Photo by author.

campfire. Sometimes the day-to-day upslope and downslope winds in mountainous areas are also responsible for bending the smoke column, so this one is generally true, but only if localized wind patterns aren't messing it up.

"When leaves of the tree show you their back, rain you will no longer lack." Again this is a variation on a theme that wind blowing through leafy vegetation will turn it backwards or upside down as it gusts when a storm is brewing. This is another saying that tends to be true and is most often the case with a strong east to southeast wind in the lower 48 states. That would mean approaching low pressure and possible stormy weather.

Can a hunter really tell the temperature outside by counting the number of chirps a cricket makes in 15 seconds and adding 40 degrees to it? Yes. For a more detailed explanation of why this is I suggest you consult an entomologist, but it's one of those quirky little things of nature that does work. It might not get you the precise

It's true. The common cricket is a pretty reliable thermometer, at least within the temperatures ranges at which the insect is active. Photo by Courtney Kinard.

temperature, but it will get within a degree or three.

Not all old weather proverbs and sayings are true. There's one that claims you can tell how severe a winter will be by watching how many nuts a squirrel collects. Supposedly the more nuts collected, the worse the coming winter. In reality, the more nuts collected the fatter the squirrel will be. If you see squirrels hording massive amounts of food when you're out scouting in late summer or early fall, it might be worth a GPS waypoint to know where to bring the kids with a .22 when the small-game season starts.

As a former broadcast meteorologist, don't get me started on Groundhog Day. Groundhogs around me always see their shadow. In fact, it's the last thing they see because the shadow is created by the illumination created from the blast of my varmint rifle. As is the case with the squirrel story, longer-range forecasts based solely on the behavior of a single animal species tend not to be reliable.

Knowledge of cloud formations and the appearance of the sky is an excellent way to understand what the weather might do in the short term. Here's a look at some kinds of clouds and the weather conditions generally associated with them.

Lowering and darkening stratus clouds are a good indication that an extended period of precipitation is on the way. Light rain started falling soon after this photo was taken during a hunt on a South Texas ranch, and it continued off and on for a couple of days. Make sure you ask the guide or landowner what happens to the ground in your hunting area after a decent shot of moisture. As you can see from the inset picture above, I had quite a clean-up job on my hands after even just a short ride through Texas desert mud. Travel with pickup trucks was next to impossible for a while, and nearly as bad with ATVs. Fortunately everyone got back to camp. Both photos by author.

Broken low clouds descending on mountains or into a canyon with darker stratus clouds visible through the breaks mean precipitation is on the way. Moderate rainfall began within an hour of my snapping this picture of Yellowstone Canyon and continued all afternoon. Photo by author.

"Red in the morning, sailors take warning!" A red sunrise at Belle Fourche Reservoir north of the Black Hills. Thunderstorms moved into the area later in the day. Photo by author.

Towering cumulus is a sign of thunderstorms to come. The cloud pictured above became a tornadic storm about an hour after the photograph was taken. Photo by author.

If you see this heading your way, run for cover. It's a shelf cloud, a formation that often moves out ahead of a severe storm containing hail, high winds, heavy rain and lightning. Your time to react and move to safety is measured in minutes when you see this formation approaching. As the rattlesnake's rattle warns, "Don't tread on me," this formation is nature's way of telling you a storm is coming that you don't want to mess with. A treestand or blind is no place to be when a shelf cloud passes overhead. Photo by author.

At the time this photo was taken this thunderstorm was producing 2" hail. The hail shaft is visible at the bottom left of the storm just to the right of a faint rainbow. The tops of thunderstorms  *tend to "lean" or "point" in the direction that the storm is moving. This shot was taken facing due east, and the storm was moving southeast.* Photo by author.

If you see a rainbow to your east, chances are the rain is over and you can get on with your hunt as cloud cover to the west of you is breaking up and sunshine can be expected for the rest of the afternoon into evening. If you see a sight like this in the morning however, head back inside the tent or cabin for another cup of coffee and a round of cards. Heavy rain is nearing your location and will likely last for at least an hour. Often morning thunderstorms are an indication that you can expect more rain later in the afternoon as well. Photo taken by author near Piedmont, South Dakota.

It is said that there is a bit of truth in every legend. The same may have held true for weather proverbs at one time, and I've no doubt that many were thought to be true at the time they were thought up. But our understanding of meteorology today is far greater than it was decades or centuries ago. Once upon a time people thought that ringing church bells or firing cannons could alter the path or intensity of an approaching storm. It was once a given that the world was flat. Time and investigation have proved such ideas to be incorrect. Yet, there are sayings that have survived over the years because they are true. We may not always understand why they are, but in time perhaps we will.

There is one indisputable fact that hunter's will do well to remember. Nature talks to us. All around us are signs, signals and wonders that let us know what is happening, and what may happen in the future. We would do well to understand all we can about the messages nature gives us. Doing so will help us become better and safer hunters, more effective conservationists and better stewards of creation.

CHAPTER 9

Weather and Your Gear

My wife and I had been married less than a year when we went on our first pheasant-hunting trip with a group of guys in west-central Minnesota. She was carrying her brand new Browning BPS shotgun and made some spectacular shots. At the end of the hunt, we zipped up our guns in their cases and headed home. Arriving late in the evening, I foolishly decided to wait until the next day to clean the shotguns but then forgot to do so the following day. On the third day after the hunt, I opened the cases and, to my great disappointment, noticed that some small areas of rust and pitting were already forming on the receiver of my wife's new shotgun. There had been no precipitation the day of the hunt, but casing her cold shotgun and placing it in an inexpensive, highly breathable gun case caused condensation to form on the metal when we took the guns indoors. The rust was evidence of our inexperience and failure to understand just how rapidly the corrosion process can begin.

Every piece of hunting gear you own is vulnerable and susceptible to damage from some condition in the environment in which you hunt. Moisture, dust, mud, clingy vegetation and debris of various forms and sizes are all capable of causing some degree of harm to hunting equipment. Of these, the most obvious is moisture.

When shopping for hunting gear, be careful to consider whether the product you're interested in is waterproof or water-resistant. A water-resistant product, whether it be a GPS unit or camo jacket, can withstand limited use in a moist environment but is not intended to be submerged or exposed to water for prolonged periods of time. When considering radios, GPS units, watches and similar items,

Adequate preparation is key to success when on the hunt of a lifetime, and such hunts can often take place in extreme weather conditions. Understanding how weather affects the performance of your equipment is essential. Snow and cold didn't stop Mark Nelsen from going after this moose in Canada with his .58-caliber Hawken muzzleloader. Photo courtesy of Mark Nelsen.

Depth of water and duration of submersion both factor into the extent to which a piece of equipment is waterproof. These Alaskan Guide binoculars were fine after spending five minutes under 10 inches of water in a pond. Photo by author.

water-resistance is often defined in the owner's manual that comes with the product. In very general terms, most water-resistant products can stand up to a bit of precipitation or endure getting a liquid spilled on them so long as the exposure is short term and the excess moisture is wiped away as soon as possible. Contrary to the notion that equipment promoted as "waterproof" is impervious to moisture; there is an international scale of standards that defines "waterproof." Let's look at this a bit more closely.

Suppose you own a product promoted as being "waterproof to IPX7 standards." IP code is part of an international system intended to precisely explain how much exposure to water the object in question can withstand. IPX7 is generally accepted as meaning that the item can be immersed in up to 39 inches of water for no longer than 30 minutes and remain relatively unaffected. Your equipment is, therefore, protected from water within the limitations set forth by the IPX7 parameters.

By comparison, IPX4 means the item can be splashed with water from any angle without damage. IPX5 means the object can be sprayed with water under pressure (as from a hose) from any angle without damage resulting. But IPX 4 and IPX5 "waterproof" standards do not necessarily mean the equipment can survive immersion. Some companies claim products rated IPX8 can be submerged indefinitely and remain safe, but one has to consider that water pressure increases with depth so the depth of submersion has to factor in somewhere and the manufacturer is responsible for informing the consumer about any such limitations. The product manual should clearly define the depth and duration limits of the product's "waterproof" limitations. By way of example, there is a camcorder on the market being advertised as "waterproof," meaning it can be submerged. Close inspection of the specifications, however, indicates it can be submerged only to a depth of

Many quality optics products are advertised as waterproof, and most do very well on hunts in adverse weather. But hunters must read the owner's manual that comes with a piece of equipment to learn what limitations there are as to how much moisture the device can withstand and if there are any limits on the duration of exposure to water. Failure to understand any limitations can lead to degraded equipment performance or damage valuable gear. Photo by author.

5 ft. for up to 60 minutes. That's fine for a pool party, but not something you'd want to take scuba diving. For the deer hunter concerned about a scope, rangefinder, GPS unit, GMRS radio or binoculars, IPX7 standards should provide sufficient waterproof protection. Such gear with this rating will stand up to downpours, and even to a brief dip in a stream or lake so long as the water isn't deep and the item is recovered quickly.

When it comes to hunting clothing, waterproof means you won't get wet if the skies open up. It doesn't necessarily mean you're wearing a camo wetsuit and can get all "Navy SEALs" on the deer you hunt by popping up out of a lake and nailing a buck. Better-known waterproof membranes in hunting outfits such as GORE-TEX® and Dry-Plus® have served me well and demonstrated their capabilities to me thoroughly. I've waded through shin-high water wearing pants outfitted with these membranes cinched tight over the uppers of waterproof boots and kept my socks dry, but I wouldn't want to stop and take in the scenery from the middle of the creek while doing so.

Water-resistant hunting clothing might keep you comfortable long enough to get back to your truck in a rain shower, but it's not something I'd recommend if you plan to sit in a tree all day in the rain. It will resist water for a time, but isn't intended for long-term exposure to wet conditions. I've found that both waterproof and water-resistant outerwear do fine in snow. When it's cold enough, the snowflakes just roll off the water-resistant gear as easily as they do waterproof outerwear.

Any exposure to moisture means that equipment and clothing has to be properly cared for once you get back to lodging after a day's hunt. No matter what the

Top-notch stainless steel such as the S30V used in this Alaskan Guide knife can take a lot of abuse in the field, but if neglected over time and not properly cared for, even the best-made steel can be damaged. Photo by author.

manufacturer's boast, I wipe down everything exposed to moisture at the end of the day to play it safe. Even stainless steel knives and gun components get a rub down. Most are under the impression that stainless steel cannot rust, but it technically can under certain circumstances, most of which involve contamination of the surface metal by dirt, mud, chlorides and other substances that may contain contaminants capable of defeating stainless steel's inherently corrosion-resistant properties. An average deer hunter is likely to encounter such potential contaminants in the course of a season. I prefer to say stainless steel is corrosion-resistant and not take chances with expensive firearms or knives. Besides, I often hunt with my family, and watching me go through a cleaning ritual at the end of a soggy day of hunting instills good equipment-care habits in my children.

Veteran hunters will also tell you to beware of the dangers condensation poses to hunting equipment. This threat increases on hunts in colder weather, and is what happened to my wife's shotgun in the story that started this chapter. During such hunts, metal components on every piece of gear you carry cool down. Completely exposed gear, such as firearms, can cool to the ambient temperature of the air. Now if you're hunting all day in 20-degree weather, case your gun in the back of the pickup, drive back to a hotel room with a controlled environment of 70° with a dewpoint of 48°, what's going to happen when you bring your gun from the vehicle into the room? The cooled metal will cool the air around it to the dewpoint and condensation will form, posing a risk of rust and corrosion. Poor-quality scopes are also very susceptible to this and tend to fog up. Once optics are internally fogged, it can take days for the lenses to clear and you may be hunting with open sights for the rest of your hunt. That's one reason why I don't buy cheap optics and insist on nitrogen-purged and completely waterproof models. Be sure to inspect your

The author's Sako .30-06 required a thorough wipe-down following this successful Black Hills deer hunt in cold weather and wet snow. Photo by author.

equipment for signs of condensation before you retire for the night, and clean or wipe affected items as needed.

As for the outerwear I've worn during the day's hunt, I'll first inspect it for tears and abrasions, and then wipe off any mud or dirt. Today's low-nap high-tech material is great when it comes to resisting burs and clingy vegetation, but I always seem to find something that came along for the ride that needs removing. In the event that ice has accumulated, especially on the lower legs of pants during winter hunts, I make sure it's thoroughly melted before I do any other cleaning or touch up work. I'm not sure what the elasticity of waterproof membranes is like when frozen solid and I don't want to risk damaging gear I paid good money for. But wet and cold aren't the only means nature has of torturing good hunting equipment.

Dry weather also poses dangers to hunting gear in the form of accumulated dust and dirt. One can never know what kinds of chemicals these substances may contain when hunting in rural agricultural areas, or what exposure to them might do to a hunter's equipment. My evening cleaning procedure begins by gently rubbing down everything wood, composite and metal with a clean soft cloth. If my firearm has been fired a few times, I clean the bore. Because the actions of my guns are lightly lubricated, they're especially prone to collecting dust and dirt and might require a more thorough cleaning and re-application of light gun oil if substantial contamination is found.

If I've been hunting in heavy cover, I'll sometimes find dried bits of vegetation adhered to the lens of my scope or binoculars. This bits were likely moist when they got stuck on my lens, and then dried there. I find the key to safe removal without scratching the lens is to remoisten the debris with water, brush it loose with a lens pen, and then gently dry the lens with a special cloth I carry just for cleaning optics. For optics I always use a lens pen or manufacturer-recommended lens cloth to gently brush away any foreign material. Make certain you follow the cleaning instructions that came with gear that has glass components or a viewing screen to avoid permanently scratching such items.

Temperature has an impact on gear as well. Basic general principles of science remind us that heating an object causes it to expand at the molecular level, and cooling causes it to contract. This is most pronounced in metallic items. Usually temperatures encountered in the field by hunters will have a greater impact on the hunter than his or her equipment, but there are some important things to remember.

After a long day of glassing for game, carefully inspect the lenses of optical equipment used for dust, dirt and vegetation. Then follow manufacturer's recommendations for the removal of foreign matter to prevent lens damage. Photo by Alex Carlson.

Everyone knows that dark colors absorb heat from the sun and light colors reflect solar energy. Leaving equipment in a vehicle can have the same result as leaving it in a giant crock-pot if the outside temperature is hot enough. Leaving gear on the dashboard can be like leaving it under a magnifying glass in direct sunlight. During hunting seasons, the sun is generally lower in the sky and weather is usually not a hot as it is in the summertime. But there are days when temperatures can hit the 80s and 90s in central and southern states during deer season. I strongly recommend that, if at all possible, hunting equipment and ammunition not be left in the hot interior of a vehicle and never on the dashboard where exposure to UV rays can destroy finish and possibly impede performance.

Among the problems I've seen resulting from prolonged exposure to heat inside a car or truck are damage to a GPS

The author strongly recommends against leaving any kind of hunting equipment on the dashboard of a parked vehicle. Doing so can result in damage from heat and UV rays, and it also presents potential thieves with inviting targets. Photo by author.

viewing screen, altered performance of ammunition that was fired when it was almost to hot to hold in a person's hand, altered performance of a firearm that was also hot to the touch, greatly decreased battery performance in electronics where batteries were exposed to temperature extremes of hot and cold, and degradation of seals on optical equipment. Apart from the battery performance, all of the problems I've outlined were the result of prolonged exposure to excessive heat. That's why my new rule of thumb is not to leave hunting equipment in a vehicle's interior that's too hot for me to leave a hunting dog in.

One area I have learned not to skimp on when it comes to protecting gear from bumps, dings, moisture, dirt and other hazards is cases. You have a great deal of money invested in your firearms, optics and electrical equipment, so it only makes sense to store and transport them in something that will shelter them from the elements. I'm a big fan of hard cases, be they made of aluminum or any of the high-impact plastic or polymer materials on the market. The way I see it, if I have $800 tied up in a quality digital camera, telephoto lens and accessories, why would I choose a cheap soft-sided camera bag? Yes, hard cases do often cost more, but consider them an insurance policy that will help you enjoy your equipment longer.

It's just common sense. Proper care and maintenance of your gear before, during and after a hunt will help it perform better and last longer. And remember, your gear is always exposed to something when it's outdoors that could harm it, so be sure to inspect it closely at the end of each day of use. But exposure to various elements isn't the only thing that can impact the performance of your equipment. Things you don't see can have just as much influence.

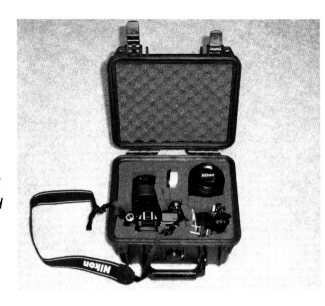

The author is a fan of quality hard cases for transporting and storing expensive equipment. For photography gear, optics and electronics, a good Pelican case is hard to beat. Photo by author.

In the chapter about wind I discussed how it can change the point of impact of a bullet downrange. But air pressure, temperature and humidity can also affect ballistics. The physics behind all of this is very complicated, and I don't want to risk writing material that would produce the same result as taking a double dose of Valium, so I'll try to keep things fairly generic.

There are several factors that determine how a bullet will fly, and two very important ones are the projectile's ballistic coefficient (BC) and its speed. The BC is simply a number calculated for a specific bullet to compare to other bullets so you know which has the higher BC, and a high BC means the bullet will fly through the air better. The higher a bullet's BC and faster its speed, the flatter the trajectory of the shot. For example, Sierra's Internet site lists the BC for its .243-caliber, 107-grain hollow point Match King bullet as being .527 moving at 2,500 fps or higher. Sierra posts the BC for its .458-caliber, 300-grain hollow point flat-nosed bullet as .120 moving at 2,400 fps. Everyone knows that the .243 is a flatter-shooting caliber than the .458, so no surprise there. What's interesting is that if you slow both those bullets down to around 1,600 fps the BC of the .243 decreases to .495 and the BC of the .458 bullet increases to .185. Why? Because there is an optimal velocity at which each bullet flies where its shape, mass and size minimize the effect of the air resistance, or drag, slowing the bullet down. There's a speed limit, if you will, beyond which it's not necessarily more productive to hurl a big blunt object or below which you lose the advantage of a smaller, thinner object. What you may not have realized is that all of these numbers are at the mercy of temperature, pressure and humidity. Now if I'm starting to lose you, just remember this: High BC is better than low BC for most longer-range shooting applications, and weather changes the BC.

When you pick up a reloading manual or a box of bullets for reloading, you'll read the bullet type and its BC. The listed BC is arrived at using factors in an international standards system and, in the absence of a velocity, assumes a temperature of 59°F, barometric pressure of 29.53 and 78% humidity. Remember that barometric pressure is a measure of how dense the air is. If barometric pressure is lowered, the air is less dense and a bullet flying through air with a barometric pressure less than 29.53 will have a higher BC. The same bullet flying at the same velocity through air more dense than 29.53 will have a lower BC. Higher temperatures at a given location tend to lower atmospheric pressure and increase a bullet's BC. Colder temperatures at the same location mean more dense air and a lower BC. Notice how I said "same location" so as not to introduce pressure differentials caused by change in altitude at this point.

Changes in relative humidity also alter a projectile's BC, but do so to such a small degree that, unless you're hunting in pouring rain, the amount of water in the air has little impact on bullet flight at reasonable hunting ranges. The biggest influence on bullet flight is barometric pressure with temperature coming in second place but only because it also relates to air density. But is this all a big deal? Let's find out.

Suppose you sighted-in your rifle at a range near Madison, Wisconsin, where the elevation is about 900-ft. above sea level and the barometric pressure on the day you shot was 30.20 with a temperature of 50°F and no wind. The ammo was .30-06 loaded with Hornady 150-grain Interbond bullets and the muzzle velocity was 2,900 fps. You set your zero at 100 yards and prepared for a mule deer hunt near Laramie, Wyoming a week later at about 8,000 feet above sea level. The big day came with a temperature of 30°F, no wind and the barometric pressure was 24.80 as you started out. Soon you had a splendid buck in your scope at 300 yards coming out of a stand of pines into a meadow. You recalled from your sight-in session that your bullet would hit about a 12.5" low at 300 yards, and the shot you had on the mulie was straight and level. You held on the deer's spine even with the back of the shoulder and fired. What happened? You nailed him, about a 11.5" below the point of aim. Why? Because deer hunters don't need to be too worried about how barometric pressure can influence bullet flight at reasonable hunting ranges and elevations where most deer hunting is done.

Long-range bench rest competition shooters and hunters going way up high for bighorn sheep, mountain goats and high-altitude elk where longer shots are more common, do have cause for concern because the influence of air pressure on bullet flight really kicks in between 400 and 500 yards and gets more pronounced from there out to 1,000 yards. In the above-described scenario and

Bullet trajectories tend to be flatter at higher altitudes, but the reverse is true with a significant decrease in altitude. Photo by author.

conditions, your bullet would impact about a foot higher in Wyoming than Wisconsin at 600 yards, dropping 77" and 88" respectively below the point of aim with your 100-yard zero. You'll find a lot of discussion about temperature, humidity and pressure and their influence on ballistics when you visit Internet sites and talk forums devoted to serious long-range shooting, but the solution for the deer hunter preparing for a guided hunt of a lifetime at a location far from home that's at a different elevation is simple. Practice and sight-in at home, and then ask to check your zero again when you arrive at the outfitter's place for your hunt. Most guides will be impressed that you care enough to ask to do this, and doing so will eliminate any concerns you have about altitude and pressure influencing your accuracy. Besides, if you're going from an area of lower elevation to a higher elevation where pressure will likely be lower, if there's any change your gun will shoot a bit flatter at the higher elevation. Hornady has an excellent Internet site that includes a ballistic calculator where you can punch in the data for your load at various barometric pressures and temperatures and then print out a trajectory table. You'll find it at www.hornady.com/ballistics.

In the interest of safety I should remind you not to underestimate the impact that hunting in higher elevations has on you, yet alone your equipment. I can't tell you how

The wisest approach to concerns about how changes in barometric pressure brought about by a change in altitude might affect your bullet's flight path is to sight the rifle in before leaving on your trip, and then sight it in again upon your arrival at the hunting destination. Photo by author.

many guides and outfitters have expressed concern to me about hunters that come to the Rockies, Alaska or Black Hills from places thousands of feet lower in elevation without adequate physical preparation. Hiking the high country is hard work, even for men and women in good shape at home. The more often you can get a good aerobic workout at home before your hunt, the better the chances your hunt will be successful and safe. Sucking air at 9,000 feet isn't the time to wish you'd been better prepared, and it's awfully hard to hold steady for a 300-yard shot when you're panting like a Lab at the end of a full day of pheasant hunting.

I'd be rehashing other books and just giving you my opinion if I were to list out what I consider to be essential equipment for a deer hunt. Such listings are entirely subjective, and what I think I "need" on a trip might be very different from what you need. If you're a stalker, you already know you need to travel light. If you have an elevated blind box in south Texas larger and more lavishly furnished than the office I'm writing this book in (don't laugh, I've seen 'em), then maybe a portable TV is a "need" for you as you wait for sundown on game day. The basics we all need are comfortable footwear for the weather predicted and style we hunt; clothing to stay comfortable, dry, concealed and sheltered from the elements; a weapon to harvest the deer with appropriate projectiles; a sharp knife; water to stay hydrated; and a valid hunting license. Other than that, the rest is pretty much optional. But realize that nature isn't forgiving and weather is her big club. Make sure you're well equipped enough to keep from tempting her to thump you on the noggin, and understand how your gear performs in various weather conditions.

CHAPTER 10

Using Weather to Your Advantage

Preceding chapters have contained a lot of information about the ways weather can influence the behavior of game, change hunting conditions, challenge hunters physically and mentally, and affect the performance of equipment. Now let's see how much of the information you've been able to retain and how to apply it during big-game hunting adventures. I'll create a hunting scenario, you decide the best strategy or course of action in that scenario, and then we'll review the situation.

It's an early muzzleloader Kansas whitetail hunt, and there are some monster bucks known to be on the land you've been given permission to hunt. The property is a mix of farm fields, most of which are loaded with alfalfa, and a small river meanders through it. You arrive at your destination only to find the weather downright hot and the warm spell is expected to continue during the duration of your stay. Highs will be in the 80s and low 90s with the forecast calling for light winds and a slight chance of afternoon and evening thunderstorms. The host has provided a number of elevated permanent stands for your use, but you have permission to hunt anywhere you like on the property. How will you proceed with the hunt?

All of the key habitat elements a big deer needs are present. There are water, food, space, cover and a desirable arrangement of each. On the first day of the hunt you rise early to get to a stand mounted at the edge of a line of trees overlooking an alfalfa field well before sunrise. As first faint light dawn arrives, all you see are deer in the distance melting into the cover that surrounds the field. No deer are seen for the rest of the day. As the last minutes of legal shooting arrive, you begin to notice deer emerging from cover and heading into the field, but a shot does not present itself before dark.

Much of the second day follows the same script from the first day until the last hour of sunlight. It's been a hot and frustrating day in the stand, but suddenly you catch movement out of the corner of your eye near the cover that marks the edge of the river bottoms. It's a dandy buck, but he's moving slow and not necessarily in your direction. What would you do?

In our section on hot-weather hunting I shared my discovery that whitetails remain relatively inactive during daytime hours when it's hot. I also wrote about my experience in finally finding deer bedded down in shade and tall grass very close to water, and that stand hunting in hot weather during all but the first and last hour of daylight can be a frustrating, low-percentage-of-success proposition. In hot weather, I go to the deer because they won't be moving much or stay too far from water in the heat of the day. On both the days described above, once the sun was up I'd head for the cover offered by the river bottoms and do a very slow spot-and-stalk hunt. Given the scenario

The hunting scenario described was nearly identical to the one Mark Nelsen faced on the muzzleloader hunt that got him this splendid Kansas whitetail. Faced with the futility of stand hunting with daytime temperatures near 90 degrees, Mark spotted this buck coming out of the river bottoms one evening from his stand and then stalked to within 100 yards before "tipping the deer over" with "Bertha," his .58-caliber Hawken. Photo courtesy of Mark Nelsen.

described, I'd carefully leave the stand upon sighting the buck; taking great care he didn't see, hear or smell me, and then attempt to close the distance for a shot.

In our next scenario, the weather is again abnormally warm, but in spite of the temperature the rut is on in the Buffalo Gap National Grasslands of southwest South Dakota. The wide-open spaces and gently rolling terrain are covered with knee-high prairie grass interspersed with draws, washes, dry creek beds and the occasional prairie pothole pond. You and your three companions know full well that this is spot-and-stalk country populated by both mule deer and whitetails, and a typical day's hunt will mean covering miles of ground. There's a light breeze and the day dawns clear with high pressure fully in control of the atmosphere overhead. Fortune smiles on you and just 15 minutes past sunrise you spot a huge mulie buck trotting after some does about 500-yards away. Equipped with good binoculars, you and your partners notice that the deer went into an area of taller grass, but did not emerge from it onto the ridge on the opposite side. How would you hunt the buck?

Open-country deer hunting is a test of patience, strategy and skill. Hunting with a small group can greatly increase your chances of success. Focused on the does, the buck has either not seen or chosen to ignore the hunters and the first course of action would be to get everyone downwind of the deer, occasionally glassing the cover and opposite ridge to ensure the deer haven't been alerted or fled. The next step would be to slowly stalk in a line with the party of four about 40-60 yards apart, but still within clear view of one another for safety. When hunting deer abreast and advancing I recommend the hunters on either end be positioned slightly ahead of those in the middle so that instead of a straight line the formation has more of a ")" shape. Years of drive-hunting deer when I was growing up taught me that having ends slightly forward increases the chances of deer fleeing straight away instead of trying to do an end run. Slow movement is essential. You know the deer are in the cover and you want them to expose themselves but not be so alarmed as to bolt away at high speed immediately. In a perfect situation, the deer will stand up or emerge from cover to look over the situation for a second or two. Having a grunt or bleat call handy can sometimes stop a buck trotting away just long enough for the shot. In this case, you're using the wind to your advantage and moving as quietly as possible as it carries your scent and sound away from the deer. This means the deer will have to visually identify you to make an accurate

Dave Downs of Rapid City, South Dakota, was on one of the ends of the drive described. The group of deer rose up and began to trot away toward one side. Dave was on one end of the drive and was able to get the buck's attention as it attempted the end run. It stopped momentarily to look the hunter over, presenting an easy broadside shot at 80 yards. A bullet from Dave's Ruger .270 dispatched the animal. The hard part, as is often the case with prairie hunts, was dragging the brute a mile and a quarter back to the truck.

When hunting prairies and high plains for deer or antelope, a good game cart is a huge help when game is downed a significant distance from the nearest road or trail. Here the author used a cart to retrieve his antelope northwest of Laramie, Wyoming, during the 2006 season.

threat assessment, and that's when you or another in your party will have a shot.

The next hunt could be anywhere in America where cold fronts sweep in with biting winds, bitter wind chill factors and blowing snow. Preseason scouting has taught you where deer like to seek shelter when the weather gets nasty. The morning is raw with temperatures in the teens, gusty and cold northwest winds, and blowing snow. For a few minutes, you and a hunting partner discuss whether or not to proceed with the hunt. Checking the local forecast, you learn that the snow is expected to taper off and winds are to subside later in the day. You both know it will be brutal hunting, but you're well equipped with insulating layers, good gloves, warm boots and hats with ear flaps.

Do you proceed with the hunt? If so, how will the hunt be carried out?

The decision about whether or not to proceed with a hunt in such conditions is entirely up to the individuals involved and depends on their level of experience, degree of preparedness and understanding of the risks. There is certainly no margin for error with dangerously cold conditions and if either hunter has reservations, the hunt should be postponed. If both are in agreement to proceed, the strategy is pretty straightforward. The deer will be seeking shelter away from open areas until the storm subsides. If preferred bedding areas are known in advance, the hunt could be over quickly. One hunter will likely need to push through the cover in hopes of jumping a deer and will be walking into the wind toward a known hiding place. The other will want to be positioned some distance due north or east of the bedding area so his scent is carried away from and not into any deer that may

"It was around 15°F, very windy and we had blowing snow. The Pennsylvania rifle season was in its second week, so the deer were in little-known hidey holes, and laying low out of the gusts. I sent my friend Todd through the secluded, wind-sheltered bedding area while I watched an escape route on the other side. This deer came trotting by at 100 yards a short time later." – John Dunlap . John's .300 Remington SAUM made quick work of this thick-antlered whitetail. Photo courtesy of John Dunlap.

be hiding, and he or she must be within view of the most likely escape route. I've used these tactics many times in similar situations, and I'm not the only one who has found them successful.

Our next hunt takes place on a clear and seemingly calm fall day in the mountains of Utah. It's nearly 3:00 in the afternoon and you're on the top of a ridge with a spotting scope. Suddenly you notice a nice buck feeding on the slope below you, and then watch him bed down on the hillside. What's the best way to put the sneak on the deer?

Recall when I wrote about upslope and downslope wind components in the mountains. Since mid morning, the wind has been blowing uphill so gently you may have not even noticed it, but any minute now the upslope will reverse and become a downslope breeze. For that reason, you will not want to approach the buck from an uphill position. Instead, move as quickly and quietly as you can down to the same elevation as the buck on the hillside, but some distance to one side of him. Start a stalk across the side of the hill toward the deer. If the downslope kicks in during the stalk, your scent will be carried toward the valley and not toward the buck, as would be the case if you were to approach him from directly above.

The predawn sky is clear with stars shining brightly as you leave your home, but as you descend into the river valley where your stand is located, you notice a blanket of white. The valley is fogged in. You manage to drive to the place you normally park your truck, take out your GPS and get a fix on your blind's location. Even though you can't see more than 10 yards, you decide to try to make it to your blind. Mindful of the scent-grabbing qualities of moisture, you remove your scent-blocking outerwear from

Phil Martin was putting the sneak on this Utah mulie from above around 3 p.m. when he was busted by a group of does with the buck, quite possibly by the onset of a downslope breeze. Fortunately, Phil was in rifle range when the buck rose to flee and the hunter's marksmanship put an end to its flight. Photo courtesy of Phil Martin.

a sealed plastic container and put it on. Then you don your waterproof, scentproof boots, gloves and hat.

Your flashlight can only illuminate the ground a few feet in front of you as you make your way to toward the stand. You step carefully and take your time, not wanting the hunt to end with a nasty fall before it can even begin. After a while you're in the trees at the edge of the field you planned to hunt and breathe a sigh of relief when you glimpse the domed shape of your ground blind in the light's beam. By the time you are situated inside it's 10 minutes past the start of legal shooting hours, but you'd never know it because the fog is so thick. Gradually, the fog begins to lighten in color and you are able to make out the shapes of trees around your stand and can even see a short distance into the field. Then, about 15 yards away, the unmistakable shape of a huge whitetail emerges from the mist. He's clueless as to your presence. Recalling the lay of the land from when you set up your ground blind, you know there are no buildings or roads behind the buck for more than a mile and he's a real wall-hanger. In the scope atop your .308 rifle, the beast's vital area fills the field of view. Do you shoot?

How many elk are there in this group? Are you sure? If you had a valid license would you harvest one of these animals?
Photo by Mark Boardman.

The same group of elk with a few additions that emerged from the mist. The photos were taken with only a brief time period between shots. Now how many elk do you see? Passing on an easy shot can be hard to do, but sometimes it's the right thing to do. I tell the students in my hunter education classes that, unless being charged by a dangerous animal intent on taking his or her life, a hunter will never be in trouble for choosing not to shoot. Photo by Mark Boardman.

The choice to fire and responsibility that comes from doing so rests with every individual hunter. I can tell you I would not shoot in this situation. In the scenario described, you can't be 100% sure of what lies beyond the buck and your rifle is powerful enough for a certain pass through at the range given. Perhaps nothing is behind it and you'll have the trophy of a lifetime. But maybe there's another deer following the buck, perhaps a tractor parked in the field that wasn't there before, and maybe even another hunter lost in the fog trying to make his way to a blind or stand. Fog can also play tricks with the eye and make things seem as are they are not. Distances can be misjudged and rangefinder performance impaired. My personal choice is to hunt in fog only when I have at least a quarter mile of visibility and am clearly able to see where my bullet will hit beyond the animal I'm shooting at.

Patience on a very cold and foggy morning also paid off for avid hunter and professional videographer, Dave Downs, during a South

Derek Fortna's day began with visibility about 10 feet in dense fog. He could barely find his way to his hunting spot, but his patience was rewarded later in the day when the fog lifted and this whitetail wandered past his western Nebraska treestand. When fog "lifts" it erodes from the outer edges inward. Watch for the coloration of the fog to lighten. In most cases where the fog bank is close to the ground with clear skies above, the lightening is an indication that visibility should improve soon. Photo courtesy of Derek Fortna.

"It was opening morning of the season. There was about an inch of snow on the ground and it was cold. There was also a full moon that night, but there was a fog in the air in the morning and the deer didn't start moving until the fog had started to lift. I used a doe-in-heat call; one of those calls in a can. Man did it work! A smaller buck came to within 50 yards of me and then ran off with a real doe that came out of a ravine. I was sitting with my back to a power pole in the middle of an alfalfa field. Then I saw the buck that I would shoot coming down the same path that the smaller buck had used. I called and he made a beeline for me. At 150 yards he turned broadside and that was that. He ran about 20 yards before crashing in the bottom of a dry creek bed, and I'll tell you it was no easy chore to drag him out of there by myself."– David Downs. Photo courtesy of Dave Downs.

Dakota whitetail hunt. I'll let him tell the story in his own words.

It's bow season in Arkansas and the weather is warm and muggy as you sit in your treestand. Morning transitions into afternoon and you notice cirrus clouds overhead, followed by altocumulus clouds. Soon a dark shadow falls over your area and you hear the distant rumble of thunder. Your stand faces east and, unable to see the western horizon, you decide to play it safe and get down from the treestand to have a look around. Once at ground level, you walk to the tree line and look behind you only to see a shelf cloud formation identical to the one pictured on page 269 approaching rapidly. The nearest shelter, a farmyard with outbuildings where you parked your truck, is just under a half a mile away. Your stand is in a shelterbelt of trees about 100 yards wide and one mile long. What would be the best course of action?

Forget about running for the farmyard. You're already in range of lightning from the storm and you'd be the tallest object in the middle of a large open area. Unless you sprint very fast and leave all your gear behind, it's most likely you wouldn't make it to shelter before the gust front winds and heavy rain got to you. Take cover in the middle of the shelterbelt away from your metal stand and the taller trees. Hunker down and cover yourself and gear with whatever waterproof material you have on hand, shut off any personal electronics and hope for the best. You'll get wet, possibly hailed on and hopefully not hit by lightning or injured by a falling tree. You'd have been better off tuning into a NOAA weather radio station on a GPS or FRS/GMRS radio equipped with a NOAA receiver when you noticed clouds beginning to increase.

The weather the preceding day was very windy with falling temperatures and the barometer rising like a

A shelf cloud. Photo copyrighted by Eric A. Helgeson, www. skewphoto.com. Used by permission.

rocket. After sundown, skies became crystal clear and the winds became calm. Temperatures continued to drop. In planning the next day's hunt, you remember that the deer had likely been hunkered down waiting out the effects of the strong cold front that moved through, and with cold Canadian high pressure now in place they will likely be coming out very hungry just before sunrise. The land you hunt is pretty open and adjacent to recently harvested cornfields. What strategy will you employ?

The deer will be on the move early and heading for the cornfields looking for cobs and kernels left on the ground. You'll want to be in a sniping position covering

Former guide Paul Kaiser took this great whitetail buck on land adjacent to an eastern Colorado field of corn stubble one cold day in 2006. Photo courtesy of Kurt Kaiser.

approaches to the corn. Dress adequately to protect yourself from the cold, and be patient. There is likely to be quite a bit of deer activity going in and out of the corn stubble through the course of the day. Given the open terrain, be sure of your background, and then wait to harvest the deer you want.

Big-game hunting requires skill and knowledge in order to overcome the formidable natural defenses that animals possess. Understanding how weather influences animal behavior, and how it can affect hunters and hunting conditions, will add to a hunter's knowledge and hopefully lead to more safe and successful hunts. There are so many variables when it comes to the subject of weather alone without factoring animal behavior that it is impossible to cover every possible scenario you might face in the field. Nevertheless, I hope you have found the information that I have presented in this book interesting and that you'll consider employing some of the weather-related strategies I've suggested. Good luck next deer season! And remember to keep an eye on the sky.

IMMERSE YOURSELF IN HUNTING HERITAGE AND HOW-TOS

Bowhunting Forests & Deep Woods
by Greg Miller
Go deep with this exciting and informative guide to big woods hunting from champion bowhunter Greg Miller.
Hardcover • 6 x 9 • 240 pages 140 b&w photos
Item# BFDW • $24.95

Strategies for Whitetail
by Charles J. Alsheimer
Explore 200 brilliant photos from the field and reliable facts about rutting behavior, growth patterns, quality deer management, while you enjoy insights about the culture of hunters.
Softcover • 8-¼ x 10-7/8 192 pages• 200 color photos
Item# WTLDD • $24.99

Mapping Trophy Bucks
Using Topographic Maps to Find Deer
by Brad Herndon
Learn how to use topographical maps to effectively implement sound terrain hunting strategies, t read deer movement, and how to use the weather to your advantag
Softcover • 8-¼ x 10-7/8 192 pages • 150 color photos
Item# TRTT • $24.99

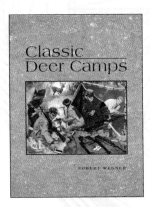

Classic Deer Camps
by Robert Wagner
Go back through time, back to the beginning of America's hunting heritage as you enjoy the spectacular collection of writings by and about hunters, including late celebrities such as Babe Ruth and Franklin D. Roosevelt.
Softcover • 8-1/4 x 10-7/8 • 224 pages 50 b&w photos • 100 color photos
Item# Z2051 • $34.99

Whitetail Wisdom
A Proven 12-Step Guide to Scouting Less and Hunting More
by Daniel E. Schmidt
If you're like many deer hunters, one of the biggest problems is finding time to get in the woods. Now, there's a book that offers easy and effective tips to make the time, and the best use of it.
Softcover • 6 x 9 • 224 pages • 110+ b&w photos • 8-page color section
Item# FTWH • $19.99